Aligning *Second Edition*

STANDARDS & CURRICULUM

FOR
CLASSROOM
SUCCESS

Aligning *Second Edition*
STANDARDS & CURRICULUM
FOR CLASSROOM SUCCESS

Daniel M. Perna
James R. Davis
FOREWORD BY FENWICK W. ENGLISH

CORWIN PRESS
A SAGE Publications Company
Thousand Oaks, CA 91320

For information:

Corwin Press
A Sage Publications Company
2455 Teller Road
Thousand Oaks, California 91320
www.corwinpress.com

Sage Publications Ltd.
1 Oliver's Yard
55 City Road
London EC1Y 1SP
United Kingdom

Sage Publications India Pvt. Ltd.
B-42, Panchsheel Enclave
Post Box 4109
New Delhi 110 017 India

Printed in the United States of America.

Library of Congress Cataloging-in-Publication Data

Perna, Daniel M.
Aligning standards and curriculum for classroom success / Daniel M. Perna,
James R. Davis. — 2nd ed.
    p. cm.
Includes bibliographical references and index.
ISBN 1-4129-4090-7 (cloth) — ISBN 1-4129-4091-5 (pbk.)
   1. Curriculum planning. 2. Education—Standards. I. Davis, James R., 1936- II. Title.
LB2806.15.P47 2007
375.001—dc22

                                        2006007589

This book is printed on acid-free paper.

06   07   08   09   10   10 9 8 7 6 5 4 3 2 1

Acquisitions Editor:	Cathy Hernandez
Editorial Assistant:	Charline Wu
Production Editor:	Jenn Reese
Copy Editor:	Cate Huisman
Typesetter:	C&M Digitals (P) Ltd.
Proofreader:	Annette R. Pagliaro
Indexer:	Jean Casalegno
Cover Designer:	Scott Van Atta

Contents

Foreword

*The Challenge of Standards
Without Standardization*

Public Law 107-110, more commonly known as No Child Left Behind (NCLB), has created a watershed in attention to the problem of instructional ambiguity in schools. While few policy developers or thoughtful administrators or teachers are opposed to educational *standards*, teachers particularly fear *standardization*. It is often hard to separate one from the other. As a practice, standardization might work if children came to school already standardized. But fortunately that is not the case. While all children are similar in some respects, they are very different in other respects. So using standards in the classroom requires knowledge of how to translate global expectations into tangible approaches, activities, and outcomes without losing the knowledge that it is the linkages between these things that are important and not a goal of simple uniformity. The trick is to be able to translate what are perceived to be rigorous goals into specific accomplishments without making each child into a replica of the others or the teacher into a robot. Already, educational researchers are picking up increasing signs of teacher alienation and burnout caused by increased accountability pressures, testing requirements, and the overuse of instructional worksheets (see Brooks, 2006).

As someone who has walked through lots of schools and visited dozens of classrooms since NCLB was passed, I am appalled at the mechanical translation of educational goals into textbook questions and vendor-produced worksheets accompanied by drill and kill approaches that leave students nearly brain-dead. I think the reader will find that Daniel Perna and James R. Davis have designed a process that respects the teacher's professionalism and works to collaborate with stakeholders in a discussion about standards and possible educational outcomes without becoming mechanical. They are not looking for recipes, but for exemplars that show teachers how to link their creative choices to standards that advance student interest and learning and that respect the teacher's choice of processes and activities as a part of goal translation. Admittedly, there is a fine line in moving to attain similar outcomes without making every teacher do it one way. Sometimes similarity of ends does have an influence on means. Over 70 years ago, John Dewey (1929) made an important distinction:

> In reality, ends that are incapable of realization are ends only in name. Ends must be framed in the light of available means. It may even be asserted that ends are only means brought to full interaction and integration. The other side of this truth is that means are fractional parts of ends. (p. 59)

What this book does is help teachers and administrators see the linkages between ends (goals) and means (activities, as in lesson plans), thereby bringing the goals to life. The approach taken also stimulates teachers to think differently about means, leading to what Dewey thought was important, that is, that the teacher is not confined to simply thinking about the improved use of old means but, rather, creates new means which will lead to enhanced learning.

There are many other complexities in promoting student success in classrooms, such as aligning assessment practices (curriculum context) with classroom practices to ensure pedagogical parallelism; understanding the role of cultural capital as creating an opportunity structure which generally favors a certain subset of privileged students, thereby expanding the achievement gap instead of shrinking it; and learning how to understand the interests of various socioeconomic classes in embracing only certain aspects of school reform while rejecting others.

But what Perna and Davis do in this text is begin the process of goal translation, from policy to practice, that is absolutely essential in working within the new constraints imposed by NCLB. The examples are concrete and should provide many teachers with workable models that will fill in the gap without leading to standardization. What is important is that the specific objectives contained within the lesson plans are not to be conceived of as static, never to be changed once promulgated. As Dewey (1929) said,

> There is no such thing as a fixed and final set of objectives, even for the time being or temporarily. Each day of teaching ought to enable a teacher to revise and better in some respect the objectives aimed at in previous work. (p. 75)

So, with this in mind, the work represented by Perna and Davis was of the continuous kind, even before NCLB teachers were engaged in it. The demands of NCLB make it more important than ever.

Fenwick W. English
R. Wendell Eaves Senior Distinguished
Professor of Educational Leadership
School of Education, University of North Carolina at Chapel Hill

References

Brooks, J. (2006). *The dark side of school reform.* Lanham, MD: Rowman & Littlefield.

Dewey, J. (1929). *The sources of a science of education.* New York: Horace Liveright.

Preface

ON THE RIGHT TRACK ■

Achieving standards should be thought of as the common destination for all students. Aligning standards to classroom practice takes time, practice, and the exercise of professional leadership and judgment. Together with members of the community, educators can construct the track on which students can travel to reach graduation and continue to learn throughout their lifetimes. If teachers are not willing or able to use standards to implement instruction, students run the risk of not meeting benchmarks, putting them behind schedule for achieving the standards or off the track completely.

Much has been written and said about standards, but there are still numerous questions about the implementation and utilization of standards in the classroom. This new edition of this book tries to provide teachers of any subject at any grade level with the tools and background to work with standards as the guiding force in their planning and course design. One of the best tools teachers can use is dialogue. The dialogue in this edition focuses on twenty-first century skills and knowledge. The book offers a structured yet adjustable way to communicate both about standards and about what students should know and be able to do in a global economy. The focus is on what students know and can do as a result of instruction, not on what the teacher will do or "cover."

Curriculum and instructional processes that educators develop through the use of this book will allow them to become and remain current in their practices. The process strikes a good balance that allows educators to design a curriculum that is unique to their school district yet does not seek to reinvent the wheel. Once educators have used this process, they will not need to start from scratch each time the instructional planning cycle begins. The product that they develop will always remain relevant through constant updating and refining.

As students travel through their school careers, they are supposed to be learning things that will help them become self-sufficient adults. Graduation standards as developed by most states, professional organizations, or local districts are the statements used to define what students should know and be able to do by the time they have completed high school so that they may be prepared for their next steps in life. To achieve conventional standards, milestones—known as *benchmarks*—are established that students must accomplish in order to demonstrate that they are proceeding along the right track toward the achievement of graduation standards. Smaller or discrete units of accomplishment at levels leading up to the benchmarks are called *criterion standards*. These criterion standards can be used to track student progress toward the ultimate goal of attaining the graduation standard.

Aligning Standards and Curriculum for Classroom Success is presented in six chapters.

Chapter 1: Student Achievement Using a Holistic Approach to Standards defines standards and discusses the strength of the standards concept. It shows how No Child Left Behind is just one factor in setting standards. The other factors—globalization, high-stakes testing, and bipartisan support for high-level skills of the future workforce—have taken standards from an idea to a solid piece of American education.

Chapter 2: The Need for Dialogue explores the necessity for dialogue among all stakeholders in the education process. Mandated state graduation standards and high-stakes testing have provided the impetus for discussion and dialogue between and among educators and noneducators about what students should know and be able to do. This chapter introduces the CAST (Communicating About Students and Teaching) dialogue process, by which individuals can come to a consensus and begin to work together as partners in education.

Chapter 3: The Language of Expectation describes how a common language can be developed so that stakeholders can come to common understandings through the use of a *verb matrix*. This matrix requires the evaluation of student performance based on Bloom's Taxonomy. When schools use the matrix, students are expected to perform beyond the memory and recall levels of learning.

Chapter 4: Designing and Using the Standards-Based Curriculum gives a step-by-step description of how state graduation standards may be translated into distinct elements—criterion standards. The chapter presents permutations of the criterion standard and shows how it can be used as a tool to unlock the power of standards. With the criterion standards, teachers, students, and parents can see the "picture" of the standard.

Chapter 5: Instructional Plans Based on Criterion Standards offers fully conceived instructional plans that begin with standards in mind. These plans are offered as a reminder that student achievement cannot be fully judged by a single event but rather must be measured during a series of opportunities for students to demonstrate what they know and can do. The majority of the plans show how standards can be integrated between subjects.

Chapter 6: Lesson Planning Takes Root offers a number of strategies for using standards to integrate the curriculum. The chapter advocates the use of the planned course document and units of instruction as a means for teachers to make evident their use of standards in their classroom practice. Summing up the sample standards-based instructional plans offered in the preceding chapters, Chapter 6 gives teachers specific means to develop their own standards-based plans for use in their classrooms.

In addition, *Resource A: Relevant Web Sites* lists sites related to standards and curriculum, and *Resource B: Verb Matrix Survey Material* includes survey materials for creating a verb matrix.

Aligning Standards and Curriculum for Classroom Success recognizes that standards are here to stay and that focusing on standards as the stimulus for and measurement of student achievement is a positive force in educational reform.

Acknowledgments

We would like to acknowledge the contributions of the following persons who provided the instructional plans used throughout this book: Brenda Lorson and Jeff Lorson, Jersey Shore Area School District; Stacey Behnert, Milton Area School District; Bryan James, Pennsylvania College of Technology; Elaine Davis, retired public school teacher and instructor at Mansfield University; Andrew Wagner, Greenwood School District; Angela Dupes, Midd-West School District; Bernadette Boerckel, James Ulrich, and Debra Fern, Warrior Run School District; Daniel S. Jury and Amy Rosenbaum, Montoursville Area School District; Crissy M. Walker, Williamsport Area School District; Rob Wallis, Muncy School District; Michael Sundberg, Mifflinburg Area School District; Charles Greco and Donna Harris, Columbia-Montour Area Vocational-Technical School; and Linda Hoover, Susquehanna Community Career and Technical Center.

In addition, we would like to thank Willard Daggett, president of the Global Center for Leadership in Education, Rexford, New York, for his help. We thank Brockway Area School District and its superintendent, Steve Zarlinsky; the elementary principal of the Mahanoy Area School District, Dr. Barbara Grazell; and the high school principal of the Moshannon Valley School District, Dr. Jack Cunning. We are very thankful to the faculty and administrators from Brockway Area School District, Mahanoy Area School District, and Moshannon Valley School District for their help in developing full K–12 curriculum documents in 2004 and 2005.

Publisher's Acknowledgments

Corwin Press gratefully acknowledges the contributions of the following reviewers:

Carol Amos, Teacher Leader and Mathematics Coordinator
Twinfield Union School, Plainfield, VT

Elizabeth Barrett, Seventh Grade Social Studies Teacher
Brian and Teri Cram Middle School, Winchester, KY

Linda Behar-Horenstein, Professor of Educational Leadership
University of Florida, Gainesville, FL

Stacy S. Carroll, Third Grade Teacher
Sedgefield Elementary, Greensboro, NC

About the Authors

 **Daniel M. Perna** is an educational consultant concentrating on school improvement and achievement. His work focuses on implementing high standards in classrooms, helping teachers develop strategies to increase student comprehension, and designing goal-oriented leadership for schools. Dr. Perna has over 30 years of experience in public education. He has been an English teacher, basketball coach, athletic director, high school principal, and assistant superintendent. He currently serves as an adjunct teacher in graduate education for Wilkes University and as an advisor to doctoral students in educational leadership at NOVA Southeastern University. He was granted a master's degree in educational administration from McDaniel College and a doctorate from NOVA Southeastern University. He has received the Pennsylvania Association of Supervision and Curriculum Directors' award for research and publications. He has presented professional development workshops, keynote addresses, and conference presentations in both the United States and in Canada. He is noted for his motivational approach to developing a passion for success in the school and classroom.

 **James R. Davis** is a retired public school administrator, thus far having spent 43 years in education, and he is still very actively involved in education as a consultant and as an advisor to doctoral students in educational leadership at NOVA Southeastern University. His educational consultant thrust concentrates on curriculum and staff development, especially as they relate to teaching and supervision in standards-based education. Dr. Davis has taught mathematics at the high school level, education at the undergraduate level, and educational administration and supervision at the graduate level. He has written articles for various educational publications, including *New Voices in Education, Education New Mexico, Pennsylvania Journal of Teacher Leadership,* and *Learning & Media.* He has received the Pennsylvania Association of Supervision and Curriculum Directors' award for research and publications. Dr. Davis earned his master's degree in guidance and counseling at Alfred University and his EdD in educational administration at New Mexico State University.

1

Student Achievement Using a Holistic Approach to Standards

For many years, the curriculum in schools has been so loosely outlined that many individual teachers have established their own ad hoc curricula. The teachers have either defined a "go as I teach" curriculum or the more common "follow the book" curriculum. These approaches have obvious repercussions. When curriculum is aligned to the preferences of a teacher or text series rather than to a set of goals mutually agreed upon by school personnel and community, one group of students may be prepared for their next level of study while another group from a different classroom at the same level in the same school may not be prepared for that level. Using standards as a framework for systematic development of curriculum will diminish the chances of a having a map for learning that is based on teacher preferences or textbook chapters. By using standards as the learning targets, the school has the opportunity to be certain that all students are moving toward the same goals, that teachers can see what they are instructionally accountable for achieving, and that students are offered support to enhance student learning.

WHAT ARE STANDARDS? ■

What standards are and what standards should be is an ongoing discussion in K–12 education. For example, Squires (2005) says that standards specify what students should know and be able to do. But O'Shea (2005) contends that standards are goals that a teacher can use to measure the success or failure of a lesson when monitoring student responses to the stated goals of the lesson. Both of these definitions fit within the boundaries of the process presented in this book. However, these very concise definitions pale when considering that states have moved beyond listing standards as a litany of simple content expectations within a traditional scope and sequence approach. States' standards are now focused on developing the higher-order assessment of knowledge as defined by Bloom's Taxonomy (Bloom, Englehart, Furst, Hill, & Krathwohl, 1956). Wiles and Bondi (2002) focus the definition of standards for this book when they state that standards have forced a move away from "mastery of low-level isolated facts to a comprehensive curriculum emphasizing problem solving, integrated tasks, real-life problems, and higher-order thinking processes using portfolios and exhibitions" (p. 305).

Standards must be explicit goals that ensure that rigorous academic content is learned in school. Standards must have quantified or qualified characteristics that inform those teaching or learning what is to be done to achieve the standard. A standard can involve one specific statement defining what a student must do to achieve it (see Figure 1.1), or it can involve a series of descriptive statements that clarifies what the student must do to achieve the level of competence expected in the standard statement (see Figure 1.2).

As one can see by the standard from Indiana in Figure 1.1, the statement is very concrete. A student is expected to read and write the numbers from 0 to 1,000,000. The statement is very specific and clear as far as assessing whether a student can do this or not. The student and teacher know the level of performance to achieve the standard.

Unfortunately, not all standards are quite so concrete. Within the myriad of state standards, there are numerous performance standards that leave room for interpretation as to what would be required to attain achievement. Therefore, neither the teacher nor the student knows exactly

Figure 1.1   A Standard as a Specific Statement

Standard: Read and write whole numbers up to 1,000,000.

SOURCE: Indiana Department of Education, 2006

Figure 1.2   A Standard as a Series of Descriptive Statements

Standard: Select and use appropriate units and tools to measure to the degree of accuracy required in particular measurement situations.

Descriptive Statements:

- Determine that a micrometer is the best tool for measuring thickness of brake pads.
- Identify the essential information for the task within the Pennsylvania Safety Code.
- Utilize the micrometer to measure the size of a brake pad on a vehicle.
- Demonstrate ability to measure the brake pad within 1/1000th of an inch.
- Interpret a chart to determine if the brakes need to be replaced.

what to do in order to measure achievement of the expectation. An example of this can be seen in this Pennsylvania standard: "Select and use appropriate units and tools to measure to the degree of accuracy required in particular measurement situations." In this case, a listing of descriptors is the only way to define what this standard actually requires. While standing alone, the standard lends itself to clarification questions, such as, "What measurement situations qualify?" or "What tools would be used to prove achievement?"

Figure 1.2 uses the Pennsylvania standard to show how a listing of expectations in relation to the original statement helps to clarify what a student could do to achieve this standard. As Kathleen Harris, who works with the Small Schools Workshops at the University of South Florida, says, "The first step in understanding standards is to draw a picture of them" (2004). What she goes on to say is that a school must determine exactly what is meant by any and all standards in the context of student achievement.

Ultimately, a standard should be one written statement or a series of statements that addresses one or more of the following:

- the level of cognitive difficulty at which a student must perform,
- the number of times a student must perform at a specified level,
- the time frame in which a student must perform at a specified level, and
- the level of teacher expectation for the performance.

The best way to align curricular objectives in terms of standards is to define the standards in terms of student performance. Perhaps the best way to accomplish this, when one statement does not define the student performance, is to render the expectations as *criterion standards.* A criterion standard is a statement listing one expectation of knowledge or performance that a student should accomplish in order to demonstrate partial achievement of a standard. The use of criterion standards recognizes that content and performance standards are two sides of the same coin and should not be thought of as separate. A standards-based curriculum should include a listing of these criterion standards. The standards on the list should reflect both the student performance expectation and the teacher content to be delivered.

The function of criterion standards is the development of a clear picture of what a student must perform in school in order to demonstrate movement toward achievement of all standards for kindergarten through twelfth grade. A strong curriculum will create a composite view in which teachers at all grades and in all courses function as team members, each making sure their respective piece of the K–12 puzzle of learning is in place at the appropriate time. In order for teachers and principals to be aware of each piece of this learning puzzle, all members of the curriculum and instructional team must have a vertical and horizontal view of the standards and their benchmarks from kindergarten through twelfth grade.

Part of putting this standards-based puzzle together is realizing that students at all levels must deal with demonstration of higher-order thinking skills. Standards statements such as "recognize change in natural and physical systems" (Pennsylvania Department of Education, 2001) require students in primary grades to do more than simply memorize content.

Instead, the youngest students are expected to make connections between content items, and a criterion standard can help to define these connections. With a standards-based curriculum, the instruction and assessment of these upper-level thinking skills are not solely the domain of the upper grades. Application, analysis, and evaluation are expected at the kindergarten or even pre-K level, and curriculum should reflect that.

For states such as Colorado, New Jersey, and Pennsylvania, where grade level is used as a benchmark to identify standards (students must have achieved certain standards by the time they finish certain grades), teachers have difficulty determining what is to be done in grades where no standards are identified. The criterion standard becomes vitally important for defining what students are expected to learn and be able to do in those grades. For example, if the state has established benchmarks at second grade and fifth grade, kindergarten through second grade teachers are responsible for the preparation to achieve the second grade benchmark while teachers in third, fourth, and fifth grade are responsible for preparing students to achieve the fifth grade benchmark. This range of grades responsible for a particular benchmark means that teachers in each grade must identify what their respective grade requires of students to move toward the instructional goal provided by the benchmarked standard.

■ BEST PRACTICES

Any educational initiative is only as good as those who practice it. Classroom teachers hold the key to the success of a standards-based curriculum. Good teachers evidence professionalism, leadership, and pedagogical expertise every day. Functioning within the framework of standards is simply another opportunity for teachers to apply their skills to positively affect student achievement. However, teachers cannot effectively and efficiently practice what has not been adequately defined. How a standard is defined can make the difference: whether the classroom professional can use the standard as a tool to achieve more positive student outcomes or whether it will confound teachers' efforts and stifle student achievement.

It is important that responsibility for the necessary instruction be placed in the hands of professional educators trained to manage the teaching and learning process. When teachers are included in the articulation and prioritization of state-mandated standards, they are able to see where they play a role in the achievement of the standards. Further, it is likely that they will feel privileged to be part of this process. Educators will know what they have to teach in order to do their parts. Yet, they will have the flexibility to accomplish this in the manner that best suits their teaching style and strengths and in a way that considers the wide range of learning styles of their students.

Since standards are actually statements of what students are supposed to know and do, teachers are now required to exercise their professional judgment as related to the expectations implied by the standards. They must continually evaluate whether individual students are progressing toward the achievement of the established standards. When a teacher recognizes that a student is falling behind, it is the teacher's responsibility to take whatever intervening steps are necessary to get the student back on track.

In order to assess fully if students are achieving the standards, the curriculum must be directly tied to daily assessment. This daily assessment can be defined in the curriculum through descriptors that identify expectations for student performance aligned to standards. This type of strong, well-enunciated, and thoughtfully written curriculum is a powerful tool for connecting what is taught to what must be assessed. A curriculum that aligns instruction with what must be tested should do the following:

- Address and reflect state standards.
- Recognize time constraints.
- Reflect local consensus and priorities.
- Seek to synchronize content areas and grade levels.
- Allow for reinforcement, reflection, and application without redundancy.
- Contain assessment possibilities within the standards themselves.

A holistic approach to standards development and student achievement results when each of the above components is present. The standards that are established, the material that is taught, and the curriculum that is assessed all will point in the same direction, toward the attainment of the expected standards.

State Standards

What becomes obvious as one examines the standards from various states is that there is no consensus from state to state as to what form standards should take (Kendall & Marzano, 1996; Schmoker& Marzano, 1999; Wiles & Bondi, 2002). Such inconsistency is antithetical to the standards movement in light of the current No Child Left Behind challenges. Both the standards movement and NCLB hold at their cores the concept of establishing rigorous standards to prepare students for competition in the twenty-first century global economy. There is the thought that having students strive to meet challenging standards will cause the competitive juices to flow between states, districts, schools, teachers, and students (Spring, 2006). However, students cannot compete fairly when each state has a different approach to designing and articulating its standards. The desire to challenge our students to meet clearly identified standards so they can be competitive in the global marketplace falters when the standards are organized and articulated in differing ways from state to state. There is no standard for standards, so there is no means by which the educational outcomes of each state can be compared in an apples-to-apples fashion.

The lack of consistency among state standards becomes evident when the levels (grades) at which the standards are to be applied is examined. In Nebraska, benchmarks adopted in 2001 for reading are established for grades one, four, eight, and twelve (Nebraska Department of Education, n.d.). However, in Pennsylvania, the benchmark levels for reading are in grades three, five, eight, and eleven (Pennsylvania Department of Education, 2001). In Indiana, there are no benchmark levels for reading.

Instead, there are English/language arts standards for every grade, and within these standards the reading standards are articulated on a continuum from kindergarten through twelfth grade (Indiana Department of Education, 2006).

More than the issue that standards cannot necessarily be contextually aligned from state to state for competitive purposes, there is a far more pertinent condition that derives from the different ways that states articulate standards. In states where there are standards statements for each grade and course, teachers know exactly what is expected for students throughout their school careers. In states where standards are benchmarked at only a few grades on the K-12 continuum, the teachers of grades for which there are no standards are left to guess what their students are expected to do.

The varying ways of establishing grade-by-grade or benchmark levels for the various standards is not the only difference in the forms that standards take. There is no nationally prescribed way of formatting standards. Some states render their standards vertically (K–12) while others render them horizontally (by subject area). This book will recommend vertical design with attention to horizontal coordination.

In Florida, Connecticut, South Carolina, Washington, and many other states, standards are accompanied by lists of student demonstrations, suggested classroom practices, and suggested parent activities (Developing Educational Standards, 2006). These differences in the way the state standards are designed show that, even though there is consensus about the need for standards, there is little consensus for how to structure a standards document. Because all states have their own standards and ways of articulating the standards, local schools and teachers need a way to develop lessons or curricula based on their own states' standards. All curriculum development should relate to state standards, and teachers, curriculum developers, and administrators need a design method for linking standards and curriculum.

Time Constraints

When the standards movement first began, researchers for Mid-continent Research for Education and Learning (McREL, formerly Mid-continent Regional Educational Laboratory) analyzed standards documents written by state boards of education and national subject area organizations and found 200 separate standards that addressed 3,093 more specific topics or benchmarks (Kendall & Marzano, 1995). They explained that a student would need to master one and one-half standards per day for 13 years in order to achieve all of the national standards. Many of the states have since determined ways to minimize the total number of standards that their students must achieve. For example, Pennsylvania has reduced the reading, mathematics, and science standards by developing what the state calls *assessment anchors* (Pennsylvania Department of Education, 2005). These assessment anchors reduce the total number of standards statements, and many of them are repeated in subsequent grades, but even with the reduction and repetition, mastering the standards is quite a challenge. A fourth grader is expected to achieve 22 standards related to mathematics, 23 standards related to reading, and 85 standards related to science. A

Pennsylvania fourth grader is expected to show proficiency with 140 standards statements in 180 days of school.

The huge number of standards and the fact that these standards are often poorly or too broadly written have led to frustration on the part of many teachers. In the days of No Child Left Behind, teachers feel compelled to be sure that students can achieve each standard because it might be tested. Beyond that, teachers struggle to determine if their interpretation of a standard is the interpretation that the state intended with the statement. If student success is the focus of a curriculum, it must be devised to help students achieve standards within a workable and worthy amount of instruction. Time is one of the most valuable instructional resources, and it must be used wisely.

Local Consensus and Priorities

The old saying that "all politics are local" holds true for all educational issues as well. There are differences in educational and funding priorities among districts within the same state, and the character and ethos of rural, suburban, and urban schools can differ greatly. Because many states leave funding of local school districts to the property taxes of those persons who reside within the district, local priorities and support are a vital and undeniable requisite for developing a standards-based curriculum. However, because student performance is measured by state testing programs, the school and the community must reach consensus on the best way to articulate local expectations of what is needed to reach the standards. Working together, educators and community members must deal with prescribed standards no matter how abundant or nebulous they may be, but the standards can provide a frame of reference within which to define what the students will be expected to do or perform during the journey through school. All of the stakeholders in the educational process must see a common goal and common purpose for this journey.

Decisions about what to include, how to cover the material, how much time to spend on the material, and how to measure a student's grasp of the material are made thousands of times every day by classroom professionals and always have been. When these professional judgments are informed by well-articulated, meaningfully defined standards, curriculum can be considered to be aligned with a clearly defined and purposeful schema. This schema can drive what the local community believes are the most important content and details that a student must possess at certain key points along the road in order to achieve the state standards.

Content Areas and Grade Levels

Both the specific content and the level at which the content is to be introduced, mastered, and then applied to new situations are often hotly debated elements when individuals are defining and interpreting what the state standards mean. What should be taught is at least as contentious as how it should be taught. What content should be taught is often seen through the prism of culture, ethnicity, and local priorities. Making the effort at the district or school level to use both subject-area experts and nonexperts from within the local school system and community can create a rigorous and, at the same time, streamlined curriculum that can deal with the exponential increase of information occurring every year. Standards are brought to life in the classroom only when the curriculum is not only defined but also organized in a manner that recognizes that precious little instructional time is available and that students need to process a massive amount of material.

Integrating the standards into curricula using tools such as curriculum mapping and thematic instruction, which have been described by Jacobs (2004), English (1999), Kovalik (1997), and Fogarty (1991), among others, can greatly enhance the chances that standards will thrive while facilitating student achievement. Much of the good presently done in classrooms is indeed appropriate and should be retained and enhanced. However, what is done must be aligned within the framework of standards. All standards must be addressed in some way in the classroom. It is impossible to teach to each individual standard. Costa (1999) suggests that teachers employ a strategy of "selective abandonment" whereby they prioritize the content that standards define. In order to do this prioritization (see Figure 1.3), Williams and Dunn (2000) and Wiggins and McTighe (2005) propose that three questions be answered: What is essential? What is supportive? What is extraneous? That which is judged to be essential should be given instructional priority; that which is supportive should be dealt with in conjunction with other material or as a cooperative or independent learning experience. The extraneous material should be included only as time allows or simply not used in instruction.

The evidence that such a method works is found in the research discussed by Reeves (2000) concerning the "90/90/90" schools. Ninety percent of students at these schools are minorities, and 90 percent of them receive free or reduced-price lunches. Yet 90 percent of these students score among the top third of students from their areas on state tests. The research shows that these schools focus on core essential expectations, use the supportive details to refine expectations, and literally refrain from dealing with the extraneous information found in the standards or written curriculum.

Reinforcement, Reflection, and Application

How teachers teach is a function of what they are asked to teach (Kovalik, 1997). Classroom professionals must engage in an ongoing dialogue about how each has a role in bringing about student achievement. Teachers can then exercise a farsighted view of what is taking place in their classrooms. When they are aware of what instruction has taken place in earlier grades and within other subject-specific classes, teachers can tailor instruction to reinforce earlier student experience, provide appropriate vehicles for students to reflect upon their prior knowledge, and support application of that knowledge in a real-world context. A clearly defined standards-based curriculum should allow for reinforcement and application without redundancy.

Assessment Possibilities

Under No Child Left Behind, states are attempting to tie their testing programs to standards, as required by federal legislation. Conceptually,

Figure 1.3   Selective Abandonment Criteria

Essential:

- Has a real-life practical application
- Is a fundamental step in a larger process
- Is based in the present
- Helps students function in the world in which they live
- Is a district- or system-articulated benchmark directly tied to a vital concept

Supportive:

- Is collaterally linked to a curricular objective
- Promotes independent study opportunity
- Can be more fully developed in another curricular area
- Provokes student interest and motivation to learn more
- Provides additional opportunities for students to develop a wide range of intelligences

Extraneous:

- Is based in knowledge about theory or the past without practical application in the future or present
- Is fun but not linked to a curricular concept
- Exercises only the logical/mathematical and verbal/linguistic intelligences
- Does not promote positive group interdependence

SOURCE: *Brain-Compatible Learning for the Block,* by R. Bruce Williams and Steven E. Dunn. ©2000 Corwin Press. Used with permission.

the standards provide a framework under which assessments can be created. The simplistic view is that if there are standards, schools can test what the standards define as necessary learning. Therefore, the teachers and the school itself can be held accountable for student achievement. Even though many teachers and administrators may question whether testing is an adequate way to appraise learning, government officials and politicians want testing as the accountability factor in creating schools for the global economy and twenty-first century. Citizens will surely compare assessment results among districts, especially when the federal government is using test data as the only gauge for determining the strongest and weakest schools in the nation.

THE CONSENSUS FOR STANDARDS   ■

The idea of and movement toward a standards-based curriculum has had a rather varied effect on teachers. Some teachers have been frustrated by the enormity of standards and the lack of direction they have been given on how to enable students to achieve them. Others believe that they should not waste their valuable time trying to conform to an idea that may be just another passing fancy of theorists, politicians, and business people. Some believe that standards will fall by the wayside as many other initiatives have when the political wind changes, and they see no need for staff development. "Why bother dealing with something that will go away?" they reason.

But standards are not going away. Standards enjoyed broad national support even prior to No Child Left Behind. In 1996, Kendall and Marzano listed no less than 17 national commissions and organizations, such as the National Committee on Science Education Standards and Assessment and the National Council of Teachers of Mathematics, as having designed national standards for their respective academic areas prior to the actual design of state standards. Each of these national groups wrote their standards with the idea that if students strive to meet the articulated standards, they will master the necessary skills within the respective disciplines. Not only is there consensus on a national level for standards, there also appears to be consensus in individual states to create standards for their respective educational programs. As one surfs the Internet to review the varied state standards, one can see that 49 of 50 states have written and adopted academic standards that define what they are expecting students to know, understand, and be able to do.

Another sign that standards are a focal point of education comes from educators and politicians who espouse the value of standards. Daggett (2003) contends that knowledge alone is inadequate and that schools must assume a leadership role in demanding that schools create higher standards so that students are challenged to meet the expectations of the workplace in the twenty-first century. The belief that seems to be defined by No Child Left Behind is that through challenging standards, educational reform will take place because the standards will force educators to examine exactly what students are supposed to know and be able to do.

As early as 1999, the American Federation of Teachers' publication *American Teacher* included an article in its December/January issue that said standards were here to stay. Since that time, we have seen adoption of and support for the basic premise of No Child Left Behind, which says each state must have standards. In November of 2004, the University of Virginia Web newsletter *Inside UVA Online* reported on a conference involving eight nationally prominent educational and political leaders. The report clearly stated that the leaders advocated modifications in programs such as No Child Left Behind, but they were unified in their belief that standards and standardized testing were not going away. A national survey of school superintendents and principals found that 87 percent of superintendents and 85 percent of principals believe that the era of testing and accountability will not end (Farkas, Johnson, & Duffett, 2003). Guskey (2005) best summarizes the issue when he points out that educators are discussing the reality of the standards movement because they are concerned with how these standards can be linked to classroom instruction so that significant improvement can occur.

Further significant evidence that standards are not going away is found in the nationwide discussion going on among noneducators. Across the United States, politicians, media sources, and the general public talk about standards. Rudalevige (2003) shows strong evidence that the concepts of standards, accountability, and testing are bipartisan issues, although there is disagreement between the parties about the nuances, funding, and who gets credit for positive models. Media writers, such as Tom Friedman in his best-selling work, *The World Is Flat* (2005), proclaim that high standards are a way to hold students and schools accountable for developing world-class students. The general public says that they want standards because the standards will provide a return on their tax dollars in the form of good schools that produce top-quality students.

With all of this said, implementing standards in the classroom remains a challenging task. Guskey (2005) points out that the focus has been on getting results rather than on developing a process of using standards to design experiences that will facilitate student learning. The writers of this book believe this is due to a lack of hands-on training to show teachers how to use the standards as a classroom tool. In many cases, it appears that standards have been designed without prior consideration of how they are supposed to be delivered and assessed in the classroom. This has contributed to the overall frustration with standards. While this frustration is understandable, poor communication should not be allowed to undermine the overall idea of an educational system based on and measured against prescribed standards. This book will help define a process for taking standards into the classroom where teachers can use standards as a focus for leading students to achievement.

STANDARDS-BASED INSTRUCTIONAL PLAN: LANGUAGE ARTS

One of the key ingredients of successfully implementing standards in the classroom is the focus on standards—each part of an instructional plan must relate to standards. Instructional plans can be written in a variety of ways; different examples are shown at the ends of each the first four chapters, and Chapter 5 includes numerous examples. The following plan, devised for primary children, connects three broadly written state graduation standards using criterion standards that relate to the elementary school level, thus aligning state standards to classroom practice.

LANGUAGE ARTS INSTRUCTIONAL PLAN

SOURCE: Brenda Lorson, Jersey Shore Area School District

Unit: **Assessing Seeds and Soils for Seed Kits**

Grade: **1**

Course: **Language Arts**

Overview of the Unit

This is a literacy experience using science content; it is an example of integrated curriculum. Students experiment with three different seeds and three different soils to decide what seeds and soils to place in their seed starter kits. The students produce a list of materials and directions for starting a seed.

Standards Assessed in This Unit

- **3.3.4.A.** Know the similarities and differences among living things.
  - ☐ List three different basic things that plants need in order to grow.
  - ☐ List the events by which a seed becomes a tree in sequential order.
  - ☐ Predict which soil the seeds will grow in best.

- **3.2.4.C.** Recognize and use the elements of scientific inquiry to solve problems.
  - ☐ Write two questions that can be answered through the investigation.
  - ☐ Create an investigation to determine which seed and soil are the best for the seed kits.
  - ☐ Write observations daily during the experiment.
  - ☐ Write a conclusion that states which type of seed and soil will be used in the seed kits, based on the results of the experiment.
  - ☐ Assess the validity of the experiment.

- **1.4.1.B.** Write informational sentences using illustrations when relevant.
  - ☐ List the materials needed for the seed kit, including which seed and soil will be added to the kit.
  - ☐ Compose a set of directions that are written in sequential order.
  - ☐ Demonstrate the use of proper capitalization, punctuation, and complete sentences.

SOURCE for standards: Pennsylvania Department of Education, 2001

Teacher Activities and Instructional Techniques

Preassessment: Ask students: What is a plant? What does a plant need in order to grow? How does a seed become a plant?

Introduction: Introduce the seed starter kit. Show students an example of a seed kit that you can buy at the store.

Reading: Read the book *The Seedling* with students.

Student Learning Activities

Preparation: Have students list three basic things that plants need in order to grow, and have them list the sequence of events by which a seed becomes a tree in sequential order.

Investigation:

1. Students write two questions that will be answered by the experiment and make a prediction about which soil is the best to grow seeds in.

2. Students create an investigation using the materials provided by the teacher: three different seeds and three different soils.

3. Students conduct the experiment for one week, writing down their observations daily.

4. Students state a conclusion from the results. They use this conclusion to determine which type of seed and soil they will use in their seed kits.

5. Students assess the validity of the experiment. For example, they might ask if the plants were watered equally or if they each received the same amount of light.

Further Activity: Have students create seed kits. The kits should include a list of materials and a set of directions for using the kit.

Measuring Achievement of Standards

Criterion Standards Rubric

1. The student listed three things that plants need to have in order to grow. YES or NO

2. The student listed the events by which a seed becomes a tree in the correct sequential order. YES or NO

3. The student predicted which soil would be the best to grow seeds in. YES or NO

4. The student wrote two questions that could be answered using the results of the experiment. YES or NO

5. The student created an investigation to determine which seed and soil to include in his or her seed kit. YES or NO

6. The student wrote daily observations during the experiment. YES or NO

7. The student wrote a conclusion that stated the type of soil and seed she or he would use in the kit. YES or NO

8. The student correctly assessed the validity of the experiment. YES or NO

9. The student correctly listed the materials needed for the seed kit, including the type of seed and soil to put in the kit. YES or NO

10. The student composed a set of directions that were written in sequential order. YES or NO

11. The student demonstrated the correct use of capitalization, punctuation, and complete sentences. YES or NO

2

The Need for Dialogue

There are great potential benefits in teachers talking with teachers from the same grade level as well as from other levels about what students really need to know and be able to do. Unfortunately, however, teachers seldom talk with one another about what students are actually doing or should be doing to learn the curriculum. Even less frequently do teachers talk about what they are doing to instruct students. When teachers do get together, they are usually involved in such things as staff development related to theoretical approaches for instruction, writing curriculum for the purpose of compliance issues, or issues of how to handle the routine activities of the school. Teachers want to talk to one another about serious pedagogical methods and basic ways to enhance what they do with students, but administrators and school boards have a tendency to say that time is too limited. When time is allotted, it is often wasted because the discussion is not structured. Currently, with No Child Left Behind, high-stakes testing, and standards, communication is critical because with the enormity of the accountability issue, teachers must decide how to maximize instruction most efficiently in a 180-day school year.

COMMUNICATING CONSENSUS ■

Certain questions are central to the challenge of designing curriculum or individual instructional units that are aligned with standards. Can a group of reasonable persons agree on what students really need to know and be able to do? Can the teacher teach everything implied in all the standards, or do groups of teachers need to define what students can learn and do within 180 days to achieve the basic concepts brought forward by the standards? This chapter endeavors to answer these questions and deal with the issues that surround the answers.

Agreeing to Agree

It is imperative that teachers communicate with each other with the expressed purpose of producing concrete results. Fullan (2000) portrayed successful schools as places where teachers meet regularly to focus on assessment and instruction. Schmoker (2002) follows that line of thinking by indicating that successful schools will inevitably see results when teachers collectively consider how to design, adapt, and assess certain standards within instruction.

Only when teachers engage in directed dialogue can standards become the focus of the curriculum being delivered in the classroom. As teachers talk about what they believe students should know and be able to do, they will discover that they already teach in alignment with many of the standards. They may also discover that they have different opinions than their colleagues regarding what must be emphasized when preparing students to meet the standards. One of the best ways to minimize varying opinions on what should be emphasized is to have a systematic approach to the dialogue. A systematic approach leads to concrete points that focus teachers on what should be learned by students at each grade level in relation to the standards.

Any dialogue process must take place before efforts at standards-based design are undertaken. As Schmoker and Marzano pointed out as early in the standards movement as 1999, "Make no mistake: The success of any organization is contingent upon clear, defined goals. A well articulated focus unleashes individual and collective energy" (1999, p. 17). The goal of dialogue should be to establish a defined focus that will unleash every participant's energy so the collective group can move in the same direction.

All teachers, administrators, and community members should be on the same page. In a recent best seller about the business world, Jim Collins (2001) points out that the best corporations know what their passion is, what they do well, and what drives them. He further discovered that strong organizations know the brutal realities about themselves. This process of discovering organizational strengths and weaknesses, as described later in this chapter, is composed of four discussion questions that lead to in-depth conversation of what it takes to build an organization that will create positive learning experiences based on standards. Each step includes an activity that leads to open and extensive exchange of philosophy and explicit beliefs about learning and students. By the time the discussion ends, there is a sense of what is really believed by the organization and what are the keys are to making the school successful in this standards-based age. In other words, the group can be focused with a passion in the realities of the school.

180 Days and Counting

The only way for the standards to be adequately addressed is for groups of teachers, administrators, and others to decide what students should do to meet the various benchmarks and standards. This means that more emphasis may be placed on certain standards than on others. Those standards that teachers agree are absolute necessities should be given the maximum amount of effort. Those that remain may be addressed in many ways, including using them as supportive criteria for achieving the emphasized standards. Some teachers may see this idea of more emphasis on some standards than others as blasphemy. However, even the most effective teachers can only deliver what they have the time to deliver. The only possible hope for actually focusing on all standards equally is through curriculum integration, and teachers need time for discussion if academic discipline barriers are ever to be removed from the delivery of curriculum. Schmoker and Marzano (1999) point out that certain standards must be emphasized over others if students are to have a chance to achieve any of the standards. If appropriate discretion is not applied, teaching to standards becomes tantamount to teaching reading by working one's way through the telephone book.

The concept that teachers must determine what standards to emphasize is provided by McTighe and Thomas (2003), Marzano (2003), and Schmoker (2002) when they suggest that keying in on important assessment objectives is the focus for achievement. They provide the evidence to support Reeves's (2000) report on the 90/90/90 schools, where there is a solidified focus on achievement of all core concepts, not a focus on coverage of standards.

The mountain of written standards makes if difficult for teachers to cover all standards within the time constraints of the school year. If teachers as a group determine which standards are the most important ones to be addressed in the time available, evidence suggests that students will score well on test questions that draw on those standards (Marzano, 2003; McTighe & Thomas, 2003; Reeves, 2000; Schmoker, 2002). There is also the possibility that by looking as a group for the standards that must be emphasized, teachers will recognize integration opportunities. By contrast, if teachers as individuals decide what to emphasize, students will not receive a consistent emphasis that will pave the way to high achievement in any of the standards. When individuals, instead of groups, determine what emphasis should be placed on standards, students are likely to receive disjunctive or repetitive instruction that hampers their ability to meet standards.

STAKEHOLDERS AS TEAM MEMBERS ■

The purpose of the aforementioned dialogue is to prepare teachers to focus on the curriculum that is actually being delivered or that should be delivered, breaking down the false perceptions of what the curriculum is as well as dealing with what teachers actually deliver. It is safe to say that even in schools where a curriculum document is in place, it is highly likely that what is outlined on the document is not what occurs in the classroom.

Contrary to what should be practiced, there is a difference between what teachers teach and what local curriculum guides articulate. Therefore, the dialogue process should begin eliciting discussion on the extent to which teachers use the local district curriculum guide as the framework for instruction. The teachers involved in the process should answer this question: "Do you use the district curriculum guide on a regular basis when planning instruction?" It is likely that most teachers will answer negatively. Some teachers may answer that they have never seen a curriculum guide; others may say that they have curriculum guides gathering dust on shelves in their classrooms. Still others may believe that the textbooks they use or state standards provide them with their curricula; therefore, they do not use the district guide.

Each of the answers is indicative of a problem with school curriculum. The curriculum guide has very little to do with what is actually taught in the classroom. Standards have the power to bring an end to the "close the door and do my own thing" manner of thinking that is detrimental to the achievement of core goals established by a written curriculum and assumed to be in place in a school. Since standards are the framework from which state-level assessments are developed, standards, curriculum, and assessment must be thought of as one in the same. By doing this, teachers prepare students for achievement of state standards.

The dialogue process then is used to help teachers begin to focus curriculum design on what students need to learn as opposed to what teachers need to teach. Because of the framework produced by standards, the content to be delivered by the teacher is evident within each standard as it is stated. How the teacher is to instruct the curriculum becomes secondary to the fact that students are assessed on the standards.

Many teachers consider curriculum a concept related to what the instructor is supposed to do. Therefore, the dialogue process is a step that helps teachers begin to refocus how they do what they do. Education is meant to provide students with the skills and knowledge they need to live successful adult lives. Therefore, education must give students the opportunity to develop skills that prepare them for life. All learning can be beneficial to a student's future life if that learning is based on the relationship standards have to the real world of living. Dialogue requires teachers to begin looking at what they teach from the perspective of how students will use the learning in their future lives.

Who Participates in the Dialogue?

Before the dialogue process can take place, people agree to take part in it as members of the dialogue team. To make the dialogue process a viable review and plan for curriculum, the dialogue team must include people who are truly interested in what students are supposed to know and be able to do. These people must be able to break from the perspective of looking at curriculum from the point of view of what the teacher is supposed to do and begin to look at curriculum from the angle of what the student is expected to do as a result of instruction. This is necessary because the standards are written from the viewpoint of what the student is supposed to know and be able to do, not what teachers are supposed to do.

The dialogue process works best with groups of people doing just what the term implies, talking. The structure of the dialogue process described here is intended to bring about the following results:

- understanding of what the term *standard* means,
- development of a strategy for facilitating student achievement, and

- determination of the core expectations that students must meet locally to achieve a standard.

For the dialogue to achieve these three things, the discussion must take place among several groups of people, including noneducators. In addition to teachers and administrators, parents and business people should participate in the dialogue process if the student achievement standards are to reflect accurately the local culture, twenty-first century skills, and the community's expectations for learning.

Teachers' Role in the Dialogue Process

Obviously, teachers are a major part of this dialogue because they work with students every day and are responsible for delivering the instruction necessary to meet the standards. Teachers who participate in a dialogue process with peers who teach at all levels, kindergarten through twelfth grade, emerge with a greater awareness that the curriculum is greater than the sum of its benchmarks. They begin to share ideas so they each know what the others are doing and recognize that each is an equal partner in helping students achieve the standards necessary for success after graduation.

Administrators' Role in the Dialogue Process

Administrators must be part of the process. The dialogue cannot consist of a meeting where administrators introduce the program and then leave the room. Because administrators are responsible for knowing what occurs in their schools, they must know what curriculum ideas are being reviewed and discussed by teachers and others. The administrators must offer their views in the conversation so that teachers know what the administrators think and believe. Also, since the administrators are those held accountable by the community when test scores or performance evaluations are reported to the public, the school leaders must be aware of the focus of the group. In addition, the administrators must clarify that teachers are expected to develop lessons based on assessment of standards and that this expectation will be part of the teacher evaluation process. Administrators may also act as facilitators in the dialogue process, informing all of the parties involved about the mandates under which the school and district function; however, when sharing ideas, administrators must be on an equal level with all participants. They cannot function as dominant players who dictate what is being done.

Parents' Role in the Dialogue Process

Parents can offer their respective interpretations of the standards as well as their views on what they believe students should learn. When parents have the opportunity to discuss curriculum with teachers, each group learns from the other. Teachers learn what parents think the school should do to educate students, and parents learn about the actual workings of the school and instruction. In addition, parents must be part of the discussion so that they begin to see how difficult it is to define what should be taught and how to teach it. They gain an understanding of the complexity of the educational process.

Business Persons' Role in the Dialogue Process

Business people can offer information about the needs of students from a corporate perspective. Since the vast majority of students will become adults who will work in some relationship with the business world, business people can help teachers and parents see what students need to know and be able to do to be productive members of society. Business people can also help the group recognize trends that may have an impact on the educational needs of the students in the future.

When educators, parents, and business people come together to discuss what is done and should be done in schools, a community consensus develops about what students should learn. Instead of having individual teachers alone deciding how standards should be addressed, the focus is broadened.

■ STEPS IN THE CAST DIALOGUE PROCESS

Communicating About Students and Teaching (CAST) is a way for the various stakeholders in the education process to reflect upon or learn about the rationale behind instruction. The steps of the process are quite simple. A teacher working alone can follow the steps, but the steps are most useful if teachers, administrators, parents, and business people join together to complete them. Each step is designed to help participants begin to recognize that there needs to be a focus on why particular information is taught. If educators are going to know how to establish a way to effectively address standards, they must have a clearly defined reason for teaching everything that they teach.

The following four questions are central to the CAST dialogue process and can help bring focus to group discussion by promoting consensus:

- Why do teachers teach what they teach?
- What is being taught?
- What standards are essential to achieve twenty-first century skills?
- How can students demonstrate what they know and can do?

Each of the four steps in the process (linked to the four focus questions above) has three discussion points: identify similarities, process apparent differences, and create a consensus statement. By talking through the discussion points and arriving at common ground at each step in the process, understanding among groups is fostered, and a true goal-oriented approach to standards can be achieved (see Figure 2.1).

Step One: Why Do Teachers Teach What They Teach?

The first step in the CAST dialogue process gets to the root of the issue. Each participant is asked to consider the following question: "Why do teachers teach what they teach?" The participants are asked to list five statements that will answer this question by completing the statement: "We teach (insert the subject to be discussed) so that students can. . . ." Participants answer this question by thinking about why an adult must

Figure 2.1 The CAST Dialogue Process

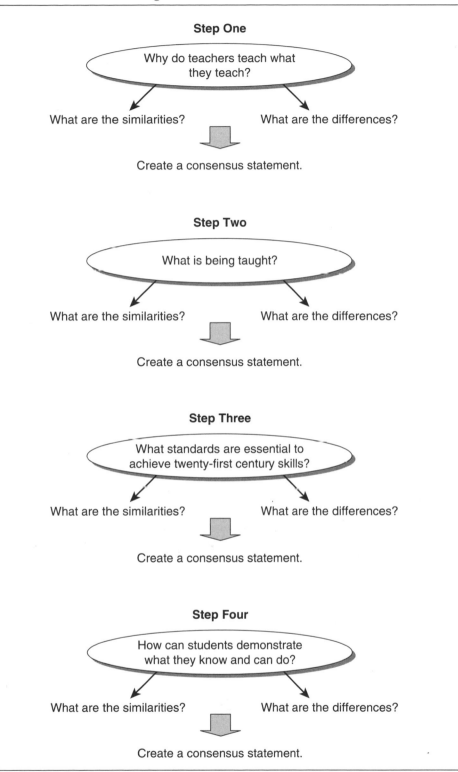

Step One

Why do teachers teach what they teach?

What are the similarities?   What are the differences?

Create a consensus statement.

Step Two

What is being taught?

What are the similarities?   What are the differences?

Create a consensus statement.

Step Three

What standards are essential to achieve twenty-first century skills?

What are the similarities?   What are the differences?

Create a consensus statement.

Step Four

How can students demonstrate what they know and can do?

What are the similarities?   What are the differences?

Create a consensus statement.

know the subject material in question. When thinking about why students are instructed in certain subjects, participants are compelled to begin thinking about why facts and concepts are really taught.

The intent is to view this question from a perspective of what people really need to know and be able to do to live productive and successful lives. The statements found on a participant's list as to why subjects are taught should give that individual and the persons with whom he or she shares his or her list an idea of the real reasons for teaching students what they are taught. Figure 2.2 lists examples of the kinds of responses that might be elicited from group discussion.

Ideally, after participants complete their lists, they should exchange or share them. Multiple perspectives have the greatest chance of bringing about understanding. Discussion should center on the various ideas presented in the lists and on how those ideas relate to students and standards. Participants can explore how people use the skills listed in their own lives, giving actual examples.

Identify Similarities

When a group is composed of persons from different groups as suggested, certain questions can lead to excellent discussion. Participants can compare lists and identify the similarities of the reasons for teaching a certain subject. They should ask themselves, "What are the similarities on the various lists?" In reviewing the examples shown in Figure 2.2, one can see that the basic concepts of addition, subtraction, multiplication, and division are taught at the elementary level, and it becomes evident from the other lists that they are the basis and foundation of other higher-order mathematical applications.

Process Apparent Differences

Another very important discussion point is the differences that exist between the lists. Participants should ask themselves, "What are the differences found in the lists?" Discussion will reveal that some persons believe teaching is done for practical living reasons, while others think teaching is done to prepare students for tests or mathematics-related functions. The obvious example of this is the high school mathematics teacher's list (see Figure 2.2). The high school teacher's list indicates that two of the reasons for teaching math are preparing students for tests and preparing students for the next level: "We teach mathematics so students can take the SATs," and "We teach mathematics so students can succeed in math courses in college." Even though both of these ideas are realistic and important, they have little to do with using mathematics as a life skill, unless one considers that getting into college provides potential life skills.

Another obvious difference is that only one individual has listed anything related to graphs and charts. Graphs and charts should be an integral part of the education of a student who will have to function in the global economy. After reviewing the concerns that Tom Friedman lays out about the competitive nature of the global economy in *The World Is Flat* (2005), we wonder how students will ever learn to compare and contrast what is happening in the world marketplace if they cannot use the higher thinking skills needed to review data from that marketplace and analyze problems by using graphs and charts as the basis for statistical analysis and reporting.

Figure 2.2   Sample Lists of Why Subjects Are Taught

Second Grade Teacher

We teach math so that students can

1. solve problems.
2. subtract.
3. measure.
4. multiply.
5. divide.

Elementary Special Education Teacher

We teach math so that students can

1. manage their finances.
2. read, understand, and interpret basic graphs.
3. use fractional parts to cook.
4. follow directions.
5. understand time and scheduling.

High School Mathematics Teacher

We teach math so that students can

1. take the SATs.
2. succeed in math courses in college.
3. have information necessary to proceed to the next level.
4. solve problems.
5. do the basic math that will be necessary when they become adults.

Parent

We teach math so that students can

1. know the numbers.
2. add, subtract, multiply, and divide.
3. use calculators.
4. control their own money.
5. use scales on a map.

Business Person

We teach math so that students can

1. complete and calculate tax responsibilities.
2. develop and follow a realistic budget.
3. make change.
4. keep accurate financial accounts.
5. make bank deposits correctly.

Create a Content-Area Mission Statement

Devising a consensus statement that addresses why the subject under discussion is taught allows for a tangible product of Step One. The conclusion should answer the question, "Why do we teach _____?"

The lists and the discussion provide the basis for creating a brief statement of why a certain subject should be taught. This statement should be no more than three sentences long and should provide the primary mission statement for the specified discipline, which then can be referred to throughout the remainder of the CAST dialogue process. This statement should be congruent with the intent of the state standards so that it is relevant to the content teachers must teach to enable students to achieve standards.

Step Two: What Is Being Taught?

In the second step of the process, teachers identify the five most important units they teach. The administrators, business people, and parents each list the five most important concepts that they believe should be taught. Once the topic and concepts are identified, there may be some specific differences among and between educators and noneducators. Our nation no longer lives in the days of the Old Deluder Satan Act when all citizens agreed that reading was important so that all students could become moral citizens via reading the Bible. Instead, we live in a day of diversity and differences (Spring, 2006; Wiles & Bondi, 2002). Because of this, we have divergent ideas about how schools are supposed to function and teach.

Even though the No Child Left Behind Act has focused on reading, mathematics, and science, there is no defined set of units or content upon which schools or community members agree. The primary example of this is the 2005 federal trial involving the Dover Area School District of Dover, Pennsylvania. The long-time argument over evolution theory versus some form of intelligent design became the focus for debate and argument over a piece of content in the district's science curriculum. This science concept has been argued over and over since the great Scopes Monkey Trial (Linder, 2002), and it provides evidence that there is a question over what the public truly believes should be taught in schools.

The differences of opinion were recognized in a study done by Daggett (2000). The study asked teachers from various disciplines to rank the importance of certain things students should be able to do while asking teachers of other disciplines, business people, and community members to rank the same expectations for learning. The data collected indicated that teachers think differently than people outside a specific discipline about what is most important. For example, of the top 10 things that the group believed students should be able to do, business leaders ranked "learning to give oral directions" as the number one expectation of English classes. Educators from fields other than English and noneducators who were not business people both rated giving directions as the third most important thing that students should be able to do. However, English teachers rated giving directions as the *ninth* most important thing students should be able to do. Teachers of specific subjects have a tendency to identify certain units as carrying more importance than those who do not teach that discipline.

Generally, teachers teach from the perspective of intellectual development. Teachers want students to know as much as possible about a subject, because the teachers love that subject. People involved in the dialogue

Figure 2.3   What Is Taught and What Should Be Taught?

The five most important units or concepts that I teach or I think should be taught are:	What is the real-world application of each of the units or concepts?

who are not attached by experience or emotion to a specific subject may help teachers understand that the primary reason for learning content should be the need to apply the content to real-life situations. Figure 2.3 can be used to record a list of the most important units and their respective real-world applications.

Participants can examine the lists using the first two discussion points presented in the CAST dialogue process: "identify similarities" and "process apparent differences." To visually represent this, participants can complete a Venn diagram to illustrate the similarities and differences. Figure 2.4 is a Venn diagram that shows the similarities and differences between lists generated by a fourth grade teacher and a business person.

Among other things, this focus question and its discussion points will likely reveal that great diversity exists, even within disciplines. But again,

Figure 2.4   Venn Diagram

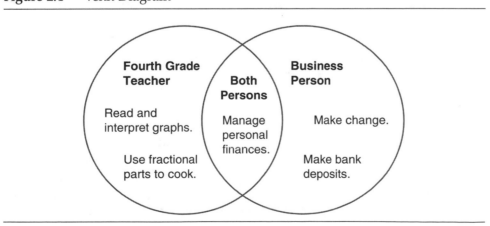

Figure 2.5   An Example of Real-World Applications Tied to Science Units

A middle school teacher listed these science units or concepts as most important:

1. Scientific Method—Use the scientific method to determine what to do about an oil spill in the ocean.

2. Land—Decide how the soil taken from the land where a new school will be built can be used.

3. Water—Explore how to help eliminate a problem of raw sewage draining into a nearby pond.

4. Environment—Determine how to use recyclable material to solve garbage disposal problems.

5. Space—Discuss how to use the sun's energy to provide energy for space travel.

it is important for participants to see common themes, even among diverse disciplines.

The ultimate real-world application comes from problem solving. In the real world, people are called upon to solve problems whose answers lie not in one content area but in the application of knowledge derived from multiple areas. Employing problem-based learning is a way to infuse authenticity into instruction and to make use of many disciplines at once. Barell defines problem-based learning as "an inquiry process that resolves questions, curiosities, doubts, and uncertainties about complex phenomena in life" (1998, p. 7).

An example of how the listing of the real-world application of units and concepts can lead to discussion is illustrated with a middle school science teacher's example in Figure 2.5.

The teacher can provide students with authentic problems to solve and facilitate the learning of units and concepts through involving the students in actually solving the problems. For example, the science teacher could involve the students in a recycling project and thereby help them learn about environmental science.

Step Three: What Standards Are Essential to Achieve Twenty-First Century Skills?

This third step in the process has two purposes: to have participants begin to consider what a student must do to achieve standards and to get participants to read and review the standards. It must be understood that many teachers and much of the public have not viewed the standards. Often standards go unused until a curriculum program is initiated or until the standards are required as part of lesson planning. This step in the CAST dialogue process asks participants to spend time reviewing the state standards that relate to the discipline under discussion and to the standards in core areas such as reading and mathematics.

After scanning the standards, several questions can lead to interesting discussion. It is important to remember at this point and at each step in the dialogue that the CAST process is meant to offer opportunities to do just that—communicate about student achievement and the teaching methods and content that need to be used and included to ensure that achievement. Standards are apparently here to stay. To keep the focus on aligning teaching with standards, discussion should not be allowed to digress into a debate about the merits of the standards movement or about the appropriateness of particular standards. There should simply be focused discussion on the standards and on what standards are important.

The focus question is, "What standards are essential for twenty-first century skills?" To begin the process of answering this question, the participants are asked to imagine that they are building a business and to identify standards that would be essential to their success. The individuals may consider any business whatsoever, so there is not a focus on only certain types of standards when the review takes place. An example of the form participants could use to accomplish this task is shown in Figure 2.6 (see pp. 28–29).

The list shown in Figure 2.6 may seem cumbersome. However, the people in the dialogue must begin to recognize that the large number of standards requires some prioritization if teachers can effectively build curriculum and instruction with standards as a focus. As they work with varied lists such as the one in Figure 2.6, all participants will begin to realize that teachers cannot possibly cover all standards. As one participant, Bob Zensinger, a very successful businessperson in Pennsylvania, said after reviewing and ranking standards, "Teachers can't possibly do all of this!"

Instead of asking what teachers should do or what the curriculum should contain, this activity requires prioritizing a list of things that students must do. Before the standards movement began, the question was, "What do the schools teach?" As the standards movement has progressed, the question has become, "What do students know and what can they do?" It becomes clear, then, that standards are not related to delivery of content but, instead, to how what has been learned will be measured. Standards have the potential to catalyze a shift in thinking for all stakeholders. The sample response shown in Figure 2.7 (see p. 29) shows how a participant still functioning under a traditional mindset lists things that the teacher is supposed to teach.

In contrast to the statements shown in Figure 2.7, the sample response shown in Figure 2.8 (see p. 29) shows that participants have taken the CAST dialogue process through the next step. Participants have started thinking about what students are supposed to do instead of thinking about what teachers are supposed to do.

Step Four: How Can Students Demonstrate What They Know and Can Do?

Step Four is a corollary to Step Three in that once one has defined the discrete skills and knowledge one should possess, the natural next step is to ask how those things can be demonstrated. There are various ways in which students can demonstrate their understanding. Perhaps the one that is most commonly employed is the test or quiz. However, paper-and-pencil examinations may do a disservice to students, because they are more likely to reveal what a student does not know than to give the student a chance to show what he or she does know. The performance assessment offers the opportunity for students to demonstrate what they can do in the context of some activity related to the intent of standards.

Figure 2.6   An Example of a Standards List From Which Participants Pick Essential Standards

Think of a business that you would like to own. As an employer in this business, place an X beside the five standards below that would be most important to you.

- **1.1.11.A.** Locate various texts, media, and traditional resources for assigned and independent projects before reading.
- **1.1.11.B.** Analyze the structure of informational materials explaining how authors used these to achieve their purposes.
- **1.1.11.C.** Use knowledge of root words and words from literary works to recognize and understand the meaning of new words during reading. Use these words accurately in speaking and writing.
- **1.1.11.D.** Identify, describe, evaluate and synthesize the essential ideas in text. Assess those reading strategies that were most effective in learning from a variety of texts.
- **1.1.11.E.** Establish a reading vocabulary by identifying and correctly using new words acquired through the study of their relationships to other words. Use a dictionary or related reference.
- **1.1.11.F.** Understand the meaning of and apply key vocabulary across the various subject areas.
- **1.1.11.G.** Demonstrate after reading understanding and interpretation of both fiction and nonfiction text, including public documents.
- **1.1.11.H.** Demonstrate fluency and comprehension in reading. Analyze the structure of informational materials explaining how authors used these to achieve their purposes.
- **1.2.11.A.** Read and understand essential content of informational texts and documents in all academic areas.
- **1.2.11.B.** Use and understand a variety of media and evaluate the quality of material produced.
- **1.2.11.C.** Produce work in at least one literary genre that follows the conventions of the genre.
- **1.3.11.A.** Read and understand works of literature.
- **1.3.11.B.** Analyze the relationships, uses, and effectiveness of literary elements used by one or more authors in similar genres including characterization, setting, plot, theme, point of view, tone, and style.
- **1.3.11.C.** Analyze the effectiveness, in terms of literary quality, of the author's use of literary devices.
- **1.3.11.D.** Analyze and evaluate in poetry the appropriateness of diction and figurative language (e.g., irony, understatement, overstatement, paradox).
- **1.3.11.E.** Analyze how a scriptwriter's use of words creates tone and mood, and how choice of words advances the theme or purpose of the work.
- **1.3.11.F.** Read and respond to nonfiction and fiction including poetry and drama.
- **1.4.11.A.** Write short stories, poems, and plays.
- **1.4.11.B.** Write complex informational pieces (e.g., research papers, analyses, evaluations, essays).
- **1.4.11.C.** Write persuasive pieces.
- **1.4.11.D.** Maintain a written record of activities, course work, experience, honors, and interests.
- **1.4.11.E.** Write a personal resume.
- **1.5.11.A.** Write with a sharp, distinct focus.
- **1.5.11.B.** Write using well-developed content appropriate for the topic.
- **1.5.11.C.** Write with controlled and/or subtle organization.
- **1.5.11.D.** Write with an understanding of the stylistic aspects of composition.
- **1.5.11.E.** Revise writing after rethinking logic of organization and rechecking central idea, content, paragraph development, level of detail, style, tone, and word choice.
- **1.5.11.F.** Edit writing using the conventions of language.
- **1.5.11.G.** Present and/or defend written work for publication when appropriate.
- **1.6.11.A.** Listen to others.

(Continued)

Figure 2.6 (Continued)

- **1.6.11.B.** Listen to a selection of literature (fiction and/or nonfiction).
- **1.6.11.C.** Speak using skills appropriate to formal speech situations.
- **1.6.11.D.** Contribute to discussions.
- **1.6.11.E.** Participate in small and large group discussions and presentations.
- **1.6.11.F.** Use media for learning purposes.
- **1.7.11.A.** Describe the influence of historical events on the English language.
- **1.7.11.B.** Analyze when differences in language are a source of negative or positive stereotypes among groups.
- **1.7.11.C.** Explain and evaluate the role and influence of the English language within and across countries.
- **1.8.11.A.** Select and refine a topic for research.
- **1.8.11.B.** Locate information using appropriate sources and strategies.
- **1.8.11.C.** Organize, summarize, and present the main ideas from research.

SOURCE for standards: Pennsylvania Department of Education, 2001.

Figure 2.7   Standard as a Series of Descriptive Statements

Proposed Standard: The teacher will prepare students to realize their full potential to acquire the knowledge and skills needed to know and use numbers, number systems, and number relationships.

Lessons will teach students the following concepts and processes: number systems, least common denominator, prime factorization, common denominator, solving simultaneous equations, number lines, graphing inequalities with domain, conjunctions, disjunctions, and quadratic equations.

Figure 2.8   A Sample Outcome for Step Four

Directions: Compose a list of five activities that students could do to demonstrate that they have achieved the following standard. What could students do to show what they know and are able to do?

Standard: Estimate, refine, and verify specified measurements of objects.

1. Identify articles in a classroom that can be measured.

2. Use floor tiles or ceiling tiles to estimate the width of the classroom.

3. Calculate the size of the classroom by using a long string.

4. Construct a box of a specific size with cardboard panels.

5. Predict the length and width of textbooks by estimating size with the length of a finger.

Even in the days of high-stakes testing, a true measure of understanding is performance in a real context, not simply recall of facts. McNamee and Chen (2005) submit that performance-based assessments complement standardized tests because the teacher is defining the steps that will be assessed to determine whether a student has met learning expectations. This concept could clearly help to define the standards that students are expected to achieve. If the standard can be identified with a real-world performance, the teachers, students, and parents know exactly what the student must do in everyday terms.

The purpose of Step Four is to have participants think in terms of how students can be assessed using activities that may have real-world implications. When the dialogue contributors think in terms of student performance as a way to learn if students are achieving standards, participants begin to recognize how many things done in schools *do* relate to the real world. The problem is that schools seldom draw the connection between what students must do in an academic sense and how this relates to the activities they must engage in as adults. There may already be consensus about what should be taught, but the participants' phrasing of what they think should be taught differs from that of others. Participants will find again that they have many ideas in common, and perhaps the apparent differences lie in the language they use to express their ideas (which leads to the next chapter where the need for a common language is discussed).

Within Step Four, participants list various ideas that they may have. These listed ideas will give the dialogue team the opportunity to discuss what has been written. Participants should look for likenesses and differences of listed activities. The group will begin to see how the ideas presented and developed demonstrate that the school does offer some real-world activities. Unfortunately, sometimes educators who work with these concepts do not think of these as real-world activities because they think in terms of instructional delivery as opposed to student performance.

As the reader may suspect from this example, participants will list activities that can be and probably are done in school. With this fourth step, however, participants in the dialogue begin to focus on how they can give students activities that are authentic. In the process of doing this, they will also recognize how standards can be assessed by student performance.

The CAST process offers the important service of giving all those who take part in it the opportunity to discuss what is happening and what should be happening within a school curriculum. The dialogue facilitates thinking in terms of student performance instead of teacher performance. The process also leads participants to think in terms of what students must do to achieve standards as opposed to what teachers must do to achieve standards. These concepts are very important in preparing people to become part of the curriculum writing necessary to devise the standards-based curriculum in a school.

■ STANDARDS-BASED INSTRUCTIONAL PLAN: U.S. HISTORY

In the following high school lesson plan, one can see that the state standards that are addressed in this lesson are broadly stated. When the standards are thus articulated, it is very important that teachers work together to determine how the more globally defined standards relate to the specificity of an instructional plan. An individual teacher's interpretation of the standards may differ from that of a colleague. When the dialogue from the first step in the curriculum design process identifies what is to be taught, and when teachers are left to create lesson plans, they can focus on how they can bring their pedagogical strengths to bear on the designated material rather than on what material to cover.

U.S. HISTORY INSTRUCTIONAL PLAN

SOURCE: Stacey Behnert, Milton Area School District

The following ninth grade American history lesson plan shows how a school has focused on a certain area of history that relates to the community's historical background with rail and river transportation. The plan includes how students are to research past events and how they are expected to compose thoughts in written form; this writing is assessed in accord with the writing standards in the state.

Unit: **Development of Transportation and Manifest Destiny**

Grade: 9

Course: US History I

Overview of the Unit

In this unit, students will explain how transportation affected the movement of Americans into western territories. Students will identify the modes of transportation of the 1800s and show how they were used with a PowerPoint presentation. Students will determine how developments in transportation changed how Americans moved.

Standards Assessed in This Unit

- **8.3.9.C.** Analyze how continuity and change have influenced United States History from 1787 to 1914.
  - ☐ Analyze how the increase of transportation routes influenced the growth of areas in the U.S.
  - ☐ Deduce how the idea of Manifest Destiny and transportation developments are connected.
  - ☐ Assess what mode of transportation was most important in the development of the U.S. in the 1800s.

- **8.1.9.C.** Analyze the fundamentals of historical interpretation.
  - ☐ Identify, using graphs, where railroad use increased in the 1800s.
  - ☐ Determine what areas of the United States saw an increase in the building of roads in the 1800s.
  - ☐ Compare and contrast water transportation to and with land transportation of the 1800s.

- **1.2.11.A.** Read and understand essential content of informational texts and documents in all academic areas.
  - ☐ Identify the different modes of transportation used in the United States in the 1800s.

☐ Explain how transportation innovations influenced the different modes of transportation.

☐ Discuss how the different modes of transportation were used and where they were used.

SOURCE for standards: Pennsylvania Department of Education, 2001

Teacher Activities and Instructional Techniques

- Monitoring of classroom and group discussions
- Facilitation of brainstorming
- Facilitation of question and answer sessions
- Demonstration of graph and map analysis

Student Learning Activities

- Completion of homework and class work
- Participation in group and class discussions
- Participation in brainstorming

Measuring Achievement of Standards

- Assessment tests
- Class and group participation
- Chart completion
- Successful completion and delivery of PowerPoint presentation

Resources

History textbooks

Various Internet resources

3

The Language of Expectation

The use of language in the curriculum development and instructional planning process is an important issue. Technical jargon and words whose meanings vary from discipline to discipline hamper the ability to connect and interact as partners in the learning process. The language of expectation for students absolutely must have clarity and definition, because it plays a significant role in defining and using standards in a meaningful way. Therefore, work with the language used to define how standards will be adopted is of the utmost importance.

THE NEED FOR A COMMON LANGUAGE ■

Peckham (1979) asserts that real meaning is demonstrated only by appropriate response. If many teachers have not appropriately responded to the challenge that standards pose, it is perhaps because the real meaning of particular standards has eluded their understanding. It follows then that teachers and all stakeholders in education can only hope to respond appropriately (by fully utilizing standards as the basis for classroom instruction) if a method to facilitate their understanding is used. Rendering state standards as criterion standards is one such method.

A Verb by Any Other Name

As uncovered in Chapter 2, standards need to be articulated and perceived as statements that identify what a student should do to demonstrate understanding. This implies student action and performance, which necessitates the appropriate and consistent use of verbs in writing standards. Stiggins's (2004) premise that verbs can activate the assessment process within the curriculum seems to agree with this contention. Verbs used in curriculum design are very important to the clarity of that design. Verbs differ from nouns in that they are not processed by the receiver as having a concrete meaning (Reyna, 1987). Teachers, students, and parents may have different visions of the meaning of many verbs.

The same idea may be extended to standards when we consider that standards and criterion standards may appear nebulous when they stand alone. The verbs used must have concrete meaning to all people using the statements. Kathleen Harris (2004) says that all "schools must draw word pictures of the standards so that all people in a school know what the standard means." Criterion standards can be used to draw this word picture. However, only concrete meanings of verbs will give the standard and the criterion standards clarity so that there is no deviation from teacher to teacher on how achievement of the standard will be assessed.

Udelhofen (2005) recommends that providing teachers with a list of action verbs that lead to higher-order thinking skills is imperative to success with standards. Her point is well made, but when a large number of verbs are simply listed as action verbs to be used when writing the word picture of standards, the chances diminish that all stakeholders are able to understand and use them in a connected manner. This chapter lays out a plan for limiting and defining such a list of verbs within the context of Bloom's Taxonomy (Bloom, Englehart, Furst, Hill, & Krathwohl, 1956). With this method, instruction is designed with content knowledge that leads to higher-order thinking. The verbs connected with the taxonomy help educators to have a sense of concrete meanings for specific verbs. Further, the placement of these verbs in each of Bloom's stratifications provides a means for instructional planners to consider creating plans that include the basic knowledge necessary to assess comprehension, application, analysis, synthesis, and evaluation.

Another reason for using a limited number of verbs within the context of Bloom is that many verbs are used for instructional planning only with respect to particular academic disciplines. The results of a dissertation study found that each academic area had a distinct list of action verbs that were used for setting learning objectives (Perna, 1997). Of 187 verbs used to define what students were expected to do when meeting learning objectives, only seven ran across all four core areas of curriculum. For the most part, each academic area had its own set of action verbs that were used to draw the word picture of what students were supposed to do to prove that they had learned something.

What can be inferred from these data is that there would likely be little consistency across the curriculum if teachers from various subject area departments sat down to write criterion standards. Teachers generally write objectives with a personal understanding of what they want students to do or to know, but such a method of writing objectives gives no assurance that others share the teacher's personal understanding of what is to be done or known. In order to bring consistency to the achievement of standards, there must be schoolwide understanding of the expectation rendered by use of a particular verb.

In addition to the potential problem that academically distinct words pose, the sheer number of verbs used can be also problematic. In the dissertation study previously cited, there were 187 verbs used by the four core subject area teachers when they wrote objectives defining student learning expectations. This mass of verbs meant there was a lack of consistency with the word picture of performance being drawn by teachers. Students were not given concrete and consistent expectations, because teachers were defining objectives with various verbs that had no specified consistent and concrete meaning from subject to subject. The only individual who knew the concrete meaning of the verb was the teacher who wrote the objective.

A lack of a limit on the number of verbs used for writing curriculum leads to performance expectations that are not consistent within the curriculum, and if performance expectations are not rendered consistently, the curriculum and assessment practices cannot be merged. Verbs have extended meanings; therefore, debating the meaning or stretching the meaning of a verb is to be expected (Reyna, 1987). However, when the school culture works from a uniform list of verbs with set definitions, there is a greater chance that responses to those verbs will be predictable across disciplines. Assessment expectations become more consistent because the verbs used to draw the word picture of the standard are consistent from teacher to teacher.

Examples of Performance Verbs That Can Cause Debate		
construct	calculate	manipulate
list	form	sort
touch	moderate	write
name	infer	identify
expound	expand	transform

There might be some consistency regarding the way verbs are used and defined within content areas. For example, all mathematics teachers use words like *add, subtract, divide,* and *multiply*. But there is little agreement among the disciplines about the meaning and use of certain verbs. This lack of horizontal continuity can limit the extent to which curriculum can be successfully integrated. For example, the word *write* was used in each of four disciplines (Perna & Davis, 1999). In communications and social studies courses, *write* always meant to compose some form of drafted statement, such as a paragraph or an essay. On the other hand, the meaning of the word *write* in mathematics and science related to the act of placing words or numbers on paper without concern for construction of a developed thought. The treatment of *write* illustrates how Peckham's (1979) theory about verbs becomes relevant. The verb *write* carried two different response expectations for students. When an English teacher asked students to write, the students were expected to develop thoughts into a coherent statement. However, when mathematics teachers asked students to write, the students were expected to respond by copying words, numbers, or geometric designs on paper without regard to developing a thought.

■ CRITERION STANDARDS AND INTEGRATED AUTHENTIC ASSESSMENT

As stated in Chapter 1, a *criterion standard* is a statement listing one expectation of knowledge or performance that a student should accomplish in order to demonstrate partial achievement of a standard Criterion standards should reflect both the student performance expectation and the teacher's approach to instruction. Wiggins and McTighe (2005), Stiggins (2004), and Schmoker (2000) all submit that the best instructional and curriculum models include defined assessments identified as a vision of expectation. A standards-based curriculum should be a listing of criterion standards in which assessment possibilities are embedded in expectations for students. A criterion standard is a statement listing one expectation of knowledge or performance that a student should accomplish to demonstrate whole or partial achievement of the more encompassing benchmark or grade-level standard.

Assessment is the process of gathering information that can be used to evaluate a student's achievement. By listing the numerous activities that a student must perform to complete a standard, the teacher can gather information about the criteria necessary for students to achieve a standard. The concept of curriculum can be tied to assessment by using a defined and prescribed list of descriptive verbs. It is probably not surprising that much of the dialogue pertaining to the use of language in curriculum development relates to the assessment methodology necessary to evaluate student performance. Wiggins and McTighe (2005) and Schmoker (2000) contend that a system of assessments should be part of instructional planning, so that tests are not arbitrary exercises done at the end of instruction. Stiggins (2004) draws curriculum planning and assessment together by indicating that quality performance criteria can be established only if assessment targets are linked directly to instructional decision making. When merging the curriculum with the assessment process, there must be consideration for several issues, which include the following:

- The curriculum must provide known and clear criteria for achievement to those assessing and those being assessed (Wiggins & McTighe, 2005).
- The heart of the curriculum must be the achievement target (Stiggins, 2004). If the teacher can locate in the curriculum exactly what is to be learned, the teacher knows exactly what the assessment should measure.

The type of assessment done in the classroom tends to be different from a standardized test. A teacher may assess a student's grasp of the rules of grammar through numerous student demonstrations of that knowledge (including writing sentences and paragraphs, speaking correctly, small tests and quizzes, and any other means by which students can show their understanding) over a sequence of several lessons. Standardized tests, however, assess competence by asking students to answer a few questions related to a given topic during a single testing event. Traditionally, most standardized tests have sought to measure only content and knowledge. However, now some state-level standardized tests seek to assess student performance by asking students to write an explanation of how they solved the problem in addition to asking for the answer to the problem.

CONSTRUCTING THE VERB MATRIX   ■

To create criterion standards that ensure consistent response to verbs, the number of verbs that curriculum designers use should be kept to a minimum. The smaller the number of verbs available, the greater the chance that people will understand the meaning of the criterion standard. Udelhofen (2005) has published a large list of action verbs that can be used in designing instruction or curriculum. Daggett (1995), Saint Edward's University Center for Teaching Excellence (2001), and the University of Maryland University College (2005) have published lists of verbs related to Bloom's Taxonomy.

Each list establishes that verbs can be used as indicators of learning expectation or performance expectation. The lists demonstrate the need to be very specific in defining how combining curriculum and assessment can be best facilitated. As stated, four of these lists base the specificity in terms of Bloom. The concepts presented in this book are very dependent on the categories of Bloom. If teachers don't understand each possible way that students can demonstrate what they have learned, students may never extend their learning beyond base knowledge. The concept of standards is that students will leave schools with applicative knowledge. This means that they comprehend what they have learned and can apply their learning in situations requiring analysis, synthesis, and evaluation.

Like the three other sources cited previously, Daggett's list (Figure 3.1) is broken down by relationship to Bloom's Taxonomy; each verb listed corresponds to a given level. For example, if the skill of analysis is to be assessed, Daggett has determined 26 different verbs used to describe analysis activities. Daggett's list of verbs is compatible with the goal of using action verbs to activate assessment possibilities within the criterion standards. Daggett's list requires people who write criterion standards to consider various components of Bloom's Taxonomy as they compose the assessment statements. Therefore, this edition of this book will continue to use Daggett's list as a tool for developing what is known as a *verb matrix.*

The reader will note that the words in Daggett's list are sorted into eight categories. Since Bloom's Taxonomy, as shown in Figure 3.2, includes only six categories, the authors of this book have modified the Daggett list to create a tool with just six categories. To do this, they have combined all the verbs listed in Daggett's categories of *comprehension, interpretation,* and *extrapolation* as verbs in the category of *comprehension* under Bloom's Taxonomy. In the first edition of this book, the authors had used the Daggett list exactly as it is shown in 3.1. However, when working with school groups and graduate students, they discovered that the *interpretation* and *extrapolation* categories only caused unnecessary work.

There are two aspects of Daggett's list that can be disconcerting to the criterion standard concept. First, as explained in the previous paragraph, it offers three groupings of verbs that all mean *comprehension.* Second, the list offers too many choices. One can see from the list that a person would

Figure 3.1 Daggett's List of Action Verbs Related to the Breakout of Bloom's Taxonomy

Knowledge Verbs

arrange	identify	choose	list	say	match	underline
reset	tally	select	touch	find	sort	omit
locate	point to	group	name	recite	label	
show	transfer	write	spell	check	cite	
hold	offer	repeat	pick	tell	quote	

Comprehension Verbs

alter	convert	qualify	retell	translate	change	expand
render	reword	vary	construct	moderate	restate	transform

Interpretation Verbs

construe	explain	infer	spell out	annotate	Define	Expound
outline	account for					

Extrapolation Verbs

advance	offer	propose	submit	calculate	contrive	project
scheme	contemplate					

Application Verbs

adopt	consume	exercise	handle	use	capitalize	manipulate
devote	exert	operate	wield	mobilize	on	
exploit	ply	put to use	profit by	employ	avail	
put in action	relate	take up	solve	try	make use of	
					utilize	

Analysis Verbs

assay	deduce	inspect	search	survey	breakdown	check
look into	section	syllogize	divide	reason	audit	dissect
canvas	examine	screen	simplify	sift	take apart	
include	scrutinize	study	uncover	test for		

Synthesis Verbs

blend	compile	create	formulate	yield	reorganize	compose
develop	generate	produce	build	originate	breed	make
reorder	cause	constitute	evolve	conceive	effect	
construct	form	mature	structure	make up	combine	

Evaluation Verbs

adjudge	award	decree	rank	settle	appraise	
censure	determine	rate	umpire	arbitrate	classify	
grade	referee	weigh	assay	criticize	judge	reject
assess	decide	prioritize	rule on			

SOURCE: Adapted from *Testing and Assessment in American Schools—Committing to Rigor and Relevance,* by Willard Daggett. ©1995 International Center for Leadership in Education, Inc. Used with permission.

have so many choices of verbs that the problem with clear meaning of verbs would not be eliminated.

Writing the Survey

Limiting the number of verbs minimizes interpretive thinking and semantic debate and offers a clearer vision of the meaning of verbs used in

Figure 3.2   Bloom's Taxonomy (1956)

knowledge

comprehension

application

analysis

synthesis

evaluation

curriculum design. To create a small number of verb choices and to create definitions for the components of the taxonomy, local input is imperative. This can effectively be accomplished by conducting a survey to determine what verbs would be best to use and how school personnel and community members perceive each component of the taxonomy. The survey can be given to teachers, administrators, students, parents, and business people throughout the school district.

The survey basically asks participants to choose a word illustration that best fits the meaning of each of the six components of the taxonomy, as shown in Figure 3.2. Then, participants are asked to choose five verbs from the list of action verbs that they believe best represent what a student could do to prove that he or she could do what the verb in Bloom's Taxonomy suggested. Figure 3.3 is an illustration of a survey sheet for the first component of Bloom's Taxonomy, *knowledge*. Additional samples can be found in Resource B.

Figure 3.3   Example of Survey Question Used to Determine the Verb Matrix

Below is the definition of *know* as stated in *Webster's New Collegiate Dictionary* (1973). Please read the definition carefully.

Know: To have direct cognition of information.

Please place a check beside the one definition that you think best fits what a student can do when the student *knows* something.

A student has direct cognition when the student

_____ 1. can communicate information or complete a learning activity without reference to external sources.

_____ 2. can use memory as the only source to answer a question or complete the steps of a task.

_____ 3. can repeat information or complete steps of a process without the use of any resource other than his or her mind and body.

_____ 4. None of the above statements is an acceptable illustration of the meaning of *know.*

If a student is expected to *know* something, which of the verbs below would best be used when asking the student to demonstrate that he or she knows the information or task process? Please circle the five verbs that you believe best illustrate the expectation.

arrange	identify	offer	repeat	spell	check	label	omit
reset	tally	choose	list	pick	say	tell	cite
locate	point to	select	touch	find	match	quote	show
transfer	group	name	recite	sort	underline	hold	write

Figure 3.4   Verb Matrix as Developed by Shikellamy School District (Sunbury, Pennsylvania)

Know: A student *knows* when the student can communicate information or complete a learning activity without reference to external sources.

| *Trigger Verbs:* | identify | list | name | state | write |

Comprehend: A student *comprehends* when the student demonstrates the nature, significance, or meaning of information by presenting the information in his or her own words.

| *Trigger Verbs:* | calculate | restate | explain | illustrate | predict |

Apply: A student *applies* learned information when the student can utilize the information in the process of solving a problem or creating a concept.

| *Trigger Verbs:* | relate | use | utilize | employ | demonstrate |

Analyze: A student *analyzes* when the student can separate the various details within a piece of information and can communicate how each detail relates to other details to form the piece of information.

| *Trigger Verbs:* | deduce | dissect | examine | break down | compare/contrast |

Synthesize: A student *synthesizes* when the student creates an idea by composing several parts and elements into one piece of information.

| *Trigger Verbs:* | combine | compose | create | develop | construct |

Evaluate: A student *evaluates* when a student can present information that supports why he or she places value or significance on pieces of information.

| *Trigger Verbs:* | appraise | assess | rate | judge | determine |

SOURCE: Shikellamy School District, Sunbury, Pennsylvania. Used with permission.

Administering the Survey

For the survey to have any statistical relevance, at least 100 people should be polled. The survey should be sent to educators (teachers and administrators), business people, and parents in equal proportions. If one chooses to survey the entire district faculty, one should endeavor to survey an equal number of business people and parents. For example, if there are 150 faculty members in a district, 150 business people should be surveyed along with 150 parents, requiring the distribution and tabulation of 450 surveys. Such a task may be too daunting in both human and material resources; therefore, a sample of 100 is adequate. Further, a school of only a few teachers can use the same survey, but these teachers must recognize that survey results may not be statistically significant.

Analyzing the Data

When analyzing the survey, the surveyors must count all the responses on all the surveys returned, and then determine which verbs have been chosen by the respondents most often. The final verb matrix is built around the verbs chosen most often by respondents. The corresponding definitions for the six components are selected in the same way. A model of a completed verb matrix is shown in Figure 3.4.

A sense of local ownership for the design of a standards-based curriculum is important, which means soliciting local input during the construction of the verb matrix. For example, the elementary teacher who constructs a matrix may want to survey his students and their parents to gather the data necessary for the matrix. The mathematics teacher in a high school may want to survey her students each year to design a verb matrix. A principal may want to survey parents and teachers to devise a matrix.

Chapter 4 describes the role of the verb matrix in the curriculum and instructional planning design process.

STANDARDS-BASED INSTRUCTIONAL ■ PLAN: MATHEMATICS

In the elementary level lesson that follows, note that the expected action is described by the verb used to start the statement, the performance verb. The performance verbs each relate to actions or demonstrations to be undertaken by the students. The assessment is built into the verb; the student either will achieve the criterion standard or will not achieve the standard. Another interesting element of this lesson is that it is to take place over the course of a year.

MATHEMATICS INSTRUCTIONAL PLAN

SOURCE: Elaine Davis, retired public school teacher and instructor at Mansfield University

Unit: **Problem Solving**

Grade: **5**

Course: **Mathematics**

Overview of the Unit

Students will participate in a discussion of problem-solving techniques and attitudes, work in small groups to solve a problem, present and defend solutions, and discuss the various ways to solve a problem.

Standards Assessed in This Unit

- **2.5.5.A.** Develop a plan to analyze a problem, identify the information needed to solve the problem, carry out the plan, check whether an answer makes sense, and explain how the problem was solved.
  - ☐ State and use the steps of the problem-solving guide to identify a problem, solve the problem, and check that the solution is reasonable.
  - ☐ List the steps of the problem-solving guide for mathematical problems.
  - ☐ Use the problem-solving guide to solve mathematical word problems.

- **2.5.5.B.** Use appropriate mathematical terms, vocabulary, language symbols, and graphs to explain clearly and logically solutions to problems.
  - ☐ Name and use appropriate mathematical terms and vocabulary (e.g., *factor, product,* etc.) to solve problems.
  - ☐ Name and use graphs and symbols to explain solutions to mathematical problems.
  - ☐ Demonstrate the ability to speak and understand the language of mathematics in explaining solutions to problems. (For example, "Factor A times factor B equals the product.")

- **2.5.5.C.** Show ideas in a variety of ways, including words, numbers, symbols, pictures, charts, graphs, tables, diagrams, and models.
  - ☐ Utilize various ways to illustrate the same information. (For example, show the information on a graph, in a table, and in a diagram.)
  - ☐ Employ a variety of methods to express ideas. (For example, use words, numbers, symbols, pictures, charts, graphs, tables, diagrams, and models.)

- **2.5.5.D.** Connect, extend, and generalize problem solutions to other concepts, problems, and circumstances in mathematics.
  - ☐ Relate known information to other problems, circumstances, and concepts in mathematics.
  - ☐ Relate a given solution to other problems, circumstances, and concepts in mathematics.

- **2.5.5.E.** Select, use, and justify the methods, materials, and strategies used to solve problems.
  - ☐ Identify and use appropriate methods to solve problems.
  - ☐ Explain methods and steps used in solving mathematical problems.
  - ☐ Employ usable methods, materials, and strategies to solve problems.
  - ☐ Demonstrate the appropriateness of selected methods, materials, or strategies used to solve problems.

- **2.5.5.F.** Use appropriate problem-solving strategies (e.g., solving a simpler problem, drawing a picture or diagram).
  - ☐ Use drawings, pictures, and diagrams as appropriate problem-solving strategies.
  - ☐ Use appropriate problem-solving strategies.

SOURCE for standards: Pennsylvania Department of Education, 2001

Teacher Activities and Instructional Techniques

1. The teacher leads a discussion of previous problem-solving sessions, which will elicit responses from students about how they felt when they first had to do problems alone, how they found out that there can be many solutions to one problem, and how important it is to have an "I can do this" attitude.

2. The teacher then tells the class a story that involves solving a problem. Students are given a written version of the story for reference while working on the problem.

3. The teacher divides the class into groups to work on the problem and then circulates among the groups, offering encouragement, asking thought-provoking questions, and providing support to students while they work on the problem.

4. The teacher selects at least one student from each group to orally present and defend a solution to the problem.

5. The teacher leads a class discussion of various solutions to the problem.

Student Learning Activities

1. Students participate in a discussion of problem-solving techniques. They discuss the various skills necessary in problem solving: reading the problem completely before starting, identifying the problem, identifying necessary information to solve the problem, developing a plan to solve the problem, organizing information, performing the mathematical operations, and developing a way of explaining and sharing the solution.

2. Students work in small groups to develop a solution to the problem. They share their individual solutions with other members of the group.

3. Student groups present and defend their solutions to the class, keeping in mind important elements of public speaking (voice, eye contact, listening to responses).

4. Students discuss the various solutions, pick one that is different from theirs, and explain why they like it and what is different about it to demonstrate their understanding that there are many ways to solve a problem, not just one "right" way.

Measuring Achievement of Standards

Preassessment

1. Students participate in a discussion of previous problem-solving activities.

2. Students contribute to a list of what they must do: distinguish relevant and irrelevant information, select a method of solving the problem, write an explanation of how they solved the problem, and orally present and defend the solution.

Formative Assessment

1. Students participate in a group while solving the problem.

2. Students show their mathematical work on a marker board.

3. Students present a solution to the class.

4. Students discuss the various solutions.

Summative Assessment

Students will be graded using the following rubric:

- Student participated in class discussions at the beginning and end of class. (15 points)
- Student worked cooperatively in a group. (15 points)
- Student solved the problem and showed work. (20 points)
- Student wrote an explanation of the problem using correct mathematical terms. (20 points)
- Student orally presented and defended a solution to the problem. (20 points)
- Student demonstrated understanding that there are various ways to solve the same problem. (10 points)

4

Designing and Using the Standards-Based Curriculum

Designing the standards-based curriculum at the district level so that it can be put to meaningful use in the classroom involves the application of some basic tools that simplify the system, but the primary action involved in this work is the thought process. To do the work of aligning curriculum to standards, analytical, interpretive, and creative thinking is required. It follows, then, that to do this well takes practice. An understanding and working knowledge of the CAST dialogue process (see Chapter 2) and the verb matrix (see Chapter 3) are important prerequisites to writing criterion standards. The dialogue process provides a means for establishing consensus and building teamwork. The decisions that are made during this process have a great potential effect on what the curriculum will ultimately look like. Designing curriculum that is standards-based using criterion standards results in having an articulated list of performance expectations that define how curriculum and instruction are directly tied to standards each time the standards are used to assess classroom learning. In addition, within the criterion standards themselves are the means for evaluating whether the standards have been met by students.

The concept of designing criterion standards from state standards is in agreement with the work done by Carr and Harris (2001), O'Shea (2005), and Squires (2005). Their work indicates that there must be teamwork, explicitly articulated expectations for using standards, and assessment in classrooms that measure student success in moving toward standards. The basic design process clearly aligns with the work of Wiggins and McTighe (2005), who define a method that they call *backward design,* and with that of Stiggins (2004), who contends that strong assessment is based on defining targets prior to instructing and assessing students. The process described in this book establishes the first step, which is setting the graduation standards as the targets. This highest level of standards provides the targets on which to focus when developing criteria at each grade level for student movement toward achievement of standards.

The process outlined in this book follows each of the three steps identified by Wiggins and McTighe (2005). They contend that after defining a desired result, there must be a determination of what evidence will be expected to prove that the desired result has been achieved. Criterion standards provide statements of what the evidence must be. Wiggins and McTighe also say that learning experiences and instruction can only be designed after one knows the results and the evidence necessary to support achievement of the results. In other words, after criterion standards are composed, teachers must decide how they will teach students to demonstrate completion of the criterion standards. Figure 4.1 expresses the relationship between graduation standards and criterion standards.

Satisfying a criterion standard is indicative of a student achieving an element of the graduation standard. The student either can or cannot listen to something and retell what was heard. The student either can or cannot employ each component of the protocol for group discussion, which is part of attaining the graduation standard. However, achievement of a standard cannot be reliably determined unless students are required to demonstrate in numerous situations, over a period of time, or within the complexity of the general expectations of the curriculum that they can do what the standard asks of them. Therefore, criterion standards must be written with enough information so that the teachers using the standards in various courses and at various grade levels know exactly what performances to assess.

Figure 4.2 shows the method by which criterion standards are derived using a process called the *standards assessment system.* With this process, local districts and schools define what local students must do in order to accomplish standards in their schools. Teachers and curriculum writers can draw upon their own experiences and information obtained from members of the community during the CAST process to determine what students need to know and be able to do in order to meet the state standard in a particular unit.

The number of criterion standards created and their level of specificity are up to those writing the statements. However, it is important to remember that one of the central components of aligning standards is making the standards easier to use in the classroom. Too much of even a good thing circumvents the purpose. Because of this, we recommend writing no more than three or four criterion standards per standard per grade, per course level, or per unit of instruction. Too many criterion standards makes it difficult to ascertain what a student must do to fulfill the rubric of expectation at a grade level, in a course, or within a unit of instruction.

Figure 4.1   Criterion Standards as Byproducts of Graduation Standards

State Standard: Listen to others.

Third Grade Benchmarks

- Listening without interrupting
- Asking clarifying questions
- Distinguishing relevant information, ideas, and opinions from those that are irrelevant
- Taking notes when prompted

Criterion Standards

1. Employs (performance verb) protocol for group discussion
   a. Utilizes (performance verb) rule of one person speaking at a time
   b. Demonstrates (performance verb) allowing all people the opportunity to speak
   c. Employs (performance verb) eye contact with speaker while listening
   d. Utilizes (performance verb) the body signals of listening
   e. Demonstrates (performance verb) proper manners when speaker makes an error

2. Composes (performance verb) questions from the oral presentation

3. Offers (performance verb) questions to the speaker

4. Retells (performance verb) ideas presented by the oral source

5. Explains (performance verb) what was presented by the oral source

6. Identifies (performance verb) reality and fantasy in the oral presentation

7. Determines (performance verb) what is reality and what is fantasy in the oral presentation

8. Identifies (performance verb) facts and opinions

9. Distinguishes (performance verb) facts from opinions

SOURCE for standard: Pennsylvania Department of Education, 2001

Figure 4.2   Constructing Criterion Standards Using the Standards Assessment System

Step One:	Review and evaluate the state standard and its benchmarks.
Step Two:	Determine the ways in which students can demonstrate that they are moving toward achievement of the standard.
Step Three:	Choose a performance verb from the appropriate level of the matrix with which to begin to write the criterion standard.
Step Four:	Compose a criterion standard that defines what students must do to be assessed in moving toward achievement of the standard.

A workable example of a criterion standard defined in terms of what students (rather than teachers) need to do is, "Students must employ protocol for group discussion," instead of "Teach students the steps of the protocol for group discussion." Using the verb matrix as a tool for writing criterion standards calls attention to the level of Bloom's Taxonomy (Bloom, Englehart, Furst, Hill, & Krathwohl, 1956) at which students are expected to function to meet the criterion standards. Writers of criterion standards decide what level of thinking is required for the student to demonstrate achievement of the standard. They make this decision by reading the definition of the key verbs and then deciding what basic things a student should be able to do to achieve the standard.

What Bloom's Taxonomy has made evident to educators for many years is that learning is not only the memory and recall of information but also the use of the higher levels of thinking. Educators should keep in mind that knowledge and comprehension alone probably will not demonstrate full achievement of a given standard. By associating the taxonomy with the achievement of standards, it becomes easier to see that by requiring students to perform at varied levels with a definite focus on the application, synthesis, analysis, and evaluation of information, students will have a greater chance of achieving the standards and growing as learners. Educators can check to see if all or most of the levels of the taxonomy are touched upon by referring back to the verb matrix and then reading the criterion standards to note their complexity. If they do not truly describe learning at the necessary level of complexity, adjustments can be made.

Sometimes the verbs alone do not guarantee that the criterion standard fits the category within which the verb is placed. As with any verb, the action is enhanced by the object or words that follow it. With this in mind, the developers of curriculum and lessons must recognize that the verbs stimulate the thinking of the writers. But the actual intent of the writer must include the necessary activity that will place a student in the higher levels of performance and critical thinking. For example, when a criterion standard says, "Create a model of a cell to use in a presentation explaining photosynthesis," the statement clearly requires the student to reach above pure memory and recall. The reader must look for this kind of complexity while using a verb from the verb matrix to kick-start thinking.

When each idea about how a student can demonstrate achievement of a particular state standard has been translated into a criterion standard, educators should reflect upon the following questions:

- Does the collection of criterion standards as they are now written require students to do more than memory and recall work?
- Does the wording of each criterion standard fulfill the expectation of the category of Bloom's Taxonomy within which it is placed?
- If a student achieves each of the criterion standards as set forth, will that mean that he or she has demonstrated movement toward achievement of the state standard?

The performance verb chosen should make what the student must know or be able to do readily apparent. Because learning is a continuum of experiences, it makes sense that teachers communicate both horizontally and vertically about what students need to know and be able to do to prepare for the next level of study and for life. For example, a third grade teacher needs to communicate with second and fourth grade teachers as well as with other third grade teachers. Thus, the achievement of standards requires a composite view of learning. The development of a standards-based model means that each grade has a part in the achievement of the standards. The groundwork for achieving standards in the twelfth grade begins in kindergarten and at home. Consequently, each grade needs a list of criterion standards to focus on with an eye to the future, toward graduation. A grade-by-grade articulation of criterion standards has the potential to dispel the misconception that only teachers at grade levels where testing takes place are responsible to prepare students to meet standards.

The process of writing criterion standards is about defining the components of learning and the possible demonstrations of that learning that are conditions of achieving the graduation standard. Recognizing that graduation standards require a continuum of performance, educators and noneducators alike can look at criterion standards and see what is expected of a student at each point in his or her education. Criterion standards are designed to tie two educational concepts together, one being state standards and the other the learning expectations of individual grade levels or courses.

WRITING CRITERION STANDARDS ■

While individual teachers can most certainly use the steps in the standards assessment system to help derive meaning from state standards documents, criterion standards written as a collaborative process in which all stakeholders take part have the most value and applicability. With this in mind, a team of persons should be formed to write the criterion standards. The objective of the writing team is to produce a document that defines exactly what students are supposed to know and be able to do. In other words, the team paints the picture of the state-mandated standards. The group develops a framework for the local district's or school's curriculum and provides evidence that the system is focusing on achievement of standards. The final picture can be used to gauge student achievement and can signal when students are not performing to expectations, so that remediation can be undertaken. The result of the team's writing and design effort will help demonstrate to the community and the state that the persons undertaking this process understand and take seriously the responsibility to prepare students to meet standards.

A crucial characteristic of the writing team is that all members are cognizant of the fact that the standards *have been determined*, and it is the team's role to decide how the district or school will address the respective standards. Members of the team must not come into this process to debate or evaluate the worth of standards. Instead, the team members must recognize the need to play the hand that they are dealt and create local pictures of the standards.

Building a Team

Selecting teams of individuals to do the writing is very important. Each team must have a writing facilitator, who typically is a teacher, curriculum coordinator, supervisor of an academic department, principal, or some other designated individual chosen by the administration. The leader's first responsibility is the selection of the group of persons who will create the criterion standards. Inclusive representation is an important consideration. Where the district is relatively small, all faculty members can participate in the process. In large districts, however, it is impractical for all faculty members to be made part of the actual writing process in some form.

Writing teams should include

- a representative from every grade level or academic discipline,
- administrators from each divisional level of the district,
- at least one guidance counselor (social workers and special education teachers may also be included or may consult on the results of the process), and
- one or two parents or businesspersons.

Persons who have served on a CAST dialogue team (see Chapter 2) can go on to serve on the writing team; however, for practicality's sake, writing teams should be smaller than dialogue teams. Subgroups formed from the dialogue teams can do the actual writing, and then the whole group can reconvene to review the writing.

Characteristics of an Effective Writing Team

Characteristics of an effective writing team are the same as those of any effective team. The working dynamic that drives this process requires that team members be cooperative and willing to recognize that debate and challenges to each other's beliefs are not negative. The team members must be able to put aside personal feelings and individual agendas in order to compromise with each other and produce the best possible product. The team must function as one unit but also be representative of all stakeholders.

It is important for people who have negative feelings about standards to work alongside those who have a more positive view. Those who are neutral on the subject should also be included. All three types are very important to the design process, because each must be heard from so that together they create a balanced view and a balanced discussion in arriving at the criterion standards.

The Textbook Dilemma

Traditionally, textbook-selection committees had a great deal of influence over what was taught and what students learned, because the materials they selected often became the de facto curriculum. It is not surprising, then, that some people want to use textbooks as a basis for writing the criterion standards. However, the use of textbooks is the wrong way to develop the criterion standards for the following reasons:

- The developed criterion standards may appear to be an outline of a textbook. This means that the local district uses the text as its curriculum rather than having a curriculum that uses the standards as its focus, thereby forfeiting the opportunity that the standards system provides to accommodate local priorities.
- Writers are likely to try very hard to write criterion standards based on an entire text rather than focusing the criterion standards on

what students must learn and demonstrate in order to show achievement of standards. The real message here is "less is more."

- Writers may rely on the text to define criterion standards instead of relying on their experience and expertise.
- Using grade- or level-specific texts hampers both horizontal and vertical efforts at curriculum integration.

Once criterion standards are defined, textbooks can be used to determine if certain concepts are missing or if the text must be mentioned in the process of writing a particular criterion standard. The textbook plays a less significant role as teachers exercise their professional skills and utilize a wide variety of instructional activities aimed at bringing about student success. The same is true with assessment, as the assessment process becomes less formal and summative than paper-and-pencil testing. Teachers choose to allow students to demonstrate proficiency in a wide variety of ways that more adequately allow for individual student differences. Assessment also becomes much more of a process and less of an event. Instruction and assessment become ongoing and intertwined. There is no longer a need for instruction to be put on hold while one tests. Articulating criterion standards makes it possible to continually assess while teaching the standards-based curriculum.

USING CRITERION STANDARDS   ■

Once graduation standards have been defined in terms of criterion standards, they can be used in many ways and by many different groups, including

- analyzing learning expectations using Bloom's Taxonomy,
- planning lessons,
- communicating expectations,
- diagnosing student learning difficulties,
- testing, and
- enhancing teacher performance.

Analyzing Learning Expectations

Once criterion standards have been written, the local entity can analyze the level of expectation that students will be required to meet. By using the relationship of action verbs to the level of learning on Bloom's Taxonomy, each criterion standard can be counted as directly relating to one level because of the performance verb that is used. For example, as Figure 4.3 shows, analysis of the Moshannon Valley School District's original work in developing mathematics criterion standards showed a heavy use of verbs at the *application* level in the taxonomy.

As the reader can see, the group that designed these criterion standards placed a very heavy emphasis on verbs from the *application* category. This may or may not be appropriate, depending upon the level and intent of the course. A high usage of one level may be desirable in specific cases. The reader is reminded of the earlier statement that suggests one must

Figure 4.3   Criterion Standards Categorized by Performance Verb Used

Number of mathematics criterion standards related to each level of Bloom's Taxonomy in Moshannon Valley School District:

Verb Category From Bloom's Taxonomy	Number of Criterion Standards Written Using Verb From the Respective Bloom Category
know	85
comprehend	66
apply	221
analyze	61
synthesize	64
evaluate	63

read an entire criterion standard in order to analyze with certainty if a statement is aligned with a particular Bloom category. Nevertheless, using the categorization from the verb matrix, a group of writers can see how they have focused on one area as opposed to another.

The reader can also note another issue the writing team will need to address. The large number of statements that have been written will create a very formidable task for the teachers and the school. When the writing group sees the actual data showing the large number of criterion statements, they may feel the need to reduce the number of expectations by either connecting one criterion statement with others or by using the verb matrix concept as a way to raise the level of expectation and thereby bring a few statements into one idea.

The Record of Knowledge

Traditional grading systems do not really tell the public what students know and can do. Many attempts have been made to reform traditional grading systems, and most have failed because there seems to be a need to give and receive A's, B's, 85's, 90's, etc. Perhaps this happens because these terms or numbers serve to rank students, and parents are familiar with the way they were graded in school. Stiggins (2004) theorizes that changing to something other than these letter and number systems may be dangerous, because the public will not understand a descriptive system.

However, the true communication of students' abilities requires a reporting system that is performance- or standards-based and actually tells parents, employers, and colleges what students know and can do. The way this is accomplished is up to the locality, but it may entail portfolios, performance checklists, projects, work samples, and rubrics. By whatever means, the key is to establish a method of communicating what the graduate actually can do. To say that the student received an A or a C in mathematics does not really tell much. Using criterion standards as a form of assessment creates a description of what students can do. Figure 4.4 shows a performance checklist for an eighth grade science student; it demonstrates how criterion standards can be used as descriptors for assessing what a student can and cannot do. To prepare reports such as that in the example, the teacher assessed students on their abilities to carry out experiments within a laboratory situation. The criterion

Figure 4.4   Performance Checklist: An Alternative to the Traditional Report Card

Grade 8 Assessment of Laboratory Experiences

Criteria	Yes	No
Defines variables	___	___
Defines controls	___	___
Identifies reason for choosing variables	___	___
Identifies reason for choosing controls	___	___
Identifies need to determine why a test must be given	___	___
Identifies inappropriate problems	___	___
Identifies correct solutions to problems	___	___
Identifies a possible solution but not a proper solution	___	___
Utilizes primary sources of information	___	___
Relates need to seek evidence to support primary sources of information	___	___
Uses complete sentences in lab reports	___	___

standards were written as part of the standards-based curriculum. The checklist documents several opportunities that students had to take part in laboratory experiences.

As the reader will note, the sample shown in Figure 4.4 allows the teacher to provide a specific breakdown of what the student can do. If a numerical or letter grading system is required, the teacher can develop a weight for each component and develop the student's grade by adding up the worth of each performance that the student has achieved. The criterion standards lend themselves to a form of rubric for every standard and every lesson, because the criterion standards define in word pictures what the student is supposed to actually achieve.

Lesson Planning

The established curriculum should be the root of lesson planning. In other words, all instruction should come out of the written curriculum. By using a standards-based curriculum designed with criterion standards, the teacher is able to design lessons directly related to state and local standards. Chapter 5 offers several standards-based instructional plans, and Chapter 6 provides a complete discussion of lesson planning with criterion standards. The plans use developed criterion standards as a basis for all lessons; therefore, all teachers, administrators, students, and community members know the source from which the lesson expectations were derived. There is no mystery or question as to why certain conditions of learning are expected; the conditional components of learning have been established through discussion and teamwork.

Communicating Expectations

One of the most obvious ways to use the criterion standards is to publish them for the entire community to see by placing them on the school's or district's Web page and in print publications such as newsletters, parent handbooks, and curriculum guides; in these ways they can be distributed to parents and businesspersons in addition to teachers and administrators. A districtwide curriculum map of standards statements is useful in communicating with staff and the public (see Chapter 6). A glance at a list of what students are supposed to know and be able to do gives interested parents and other members of the public a basic knowledge of the learning expectations of the district. The map of standards statements can provide a profile of learning expectations for graduates and for students in each grade along the way.

An effort should be made to call parents' attention to the standards and to the fact that they can monitor their children's progress against the articulated criterion standards. In addition, these statements can be used as a tool to further parent-teacher communication. When parents and interested community members read them, they can see what students are expected to achieve, as opposed to knowing only that students must take courses in particular disciplines, such mathematics, science, social studies, and English.

Diagnosing Student Learning Difficulties

When voluminous state standards documents are distilled into criterion standards, teachers have a ready checklist to use as a diagnostic tool. Criterion standards itemize what students know and can do, and they make clear what they cannot do. This allows the professional educator to identify potential problems and institute measures to remedy those problems. As diagnostic tools, criterion standards can be used in student conferences, parent conferences, and discussions or analyses of state-level tests.

Student Conferences

If the students are fully aware of what they are supposed to know and be able to do, the teacher can confer with students by using the statements as a way to discuss their strengths and deficiencies. The teacher can literally point to specific criterion standards and tell individual students whether they are meeting each standard.

Parent Conferences

The same thing can be done in parent conferences. In many school districts, teachers use the appropriate criterion standards to inform parents of what their children are doing. The criterion standards are a checklist of items to discuss with the parent, and the teacher can point out what the student can do, is close to being able to do, and is not capable of doing. This way, parents have more than a grade to use as a gauge for their children's success.

State-Level Testing

The third way that teachers can use the criterion standards as a diagnostic tool comes while preparing students for state-level testing. If teachers monitor and assess students in accordance with criterion standards, they have an abundance of evidence that tells them whether students will do well on the test. For example, if the teacher has ascertained that a student knows and can do almost all things on the criterion standard list, then the teacher can feel a sense of confidence that the student will achieve adequate scores on the assessment test. Conversely, if the teacher has determined that the student shows decided deficiencies, the teacher has a strong case for predicting that the student will have difficulty on the state assessment.

Criterion-Referenced Testing

Criterion-referenced tests are assessment tools that test only those concepts, facts, and ideas (the criteria) that students have been informed they will be tested on. Burke defines criterion-referenced tests as standardized assessments that "are designed to compare a student's test performance to learning tasks or skill levels" (1994, p. 17). The tests are most often designed by teams of teachers with input from administrators. Districts can use criterion standards they have created to devise criterion-referenced assessments. They can then test the students and gather data to measure the success of the curriculum. Such tests should be devised to assess the achievement of criterion standards exactly as criterion standards were written. Figure 4.5 provides a sample of fifth grade reading criteria that can be tested on a local basis.

This list of criteria can be used to develop a test that provides the means to gather data on each student, and also, by designing a test around the criteria, the district can gather descriptive data as to what all students can and cannot do.

An ongoing assessment program in the classroom can be criterion-based if criterion standards are prevalent. Teachers cannot afford the time to stop instruction to conduct traditional testing activities on a daily basis. However, when teachers and students enter into the instructional process with an understanding of the standards to be achieved and the procedures for assessment, teachers are encouraged to utilize their professional

Figure 4.5   Standards as a Series of Descriptive Statements

Uses prior knowledge in reading a story

Writes inferences about the title of the story

Lists valid reasons why the author wrote the story

Determines appropriate inferences from the picture

Predicts a setting correctly

Employs clues to support inferences of a character's whereabouts

Infers correctly what a character is doing

Relates clues to support inference of what a character is doing

Infers correctly the location of a character

Utilizes clues to support the inference of the character's location judgment concerning student's abilities on an ongoing basis. Therefore, criterion-referenced assessment can take place every day, because students are engaged in daily activities designed to determine if students can meet the criterion standard expectation.

Teaching to the test is not bad. In fact, if assessments are practical and appropriate, teaching to such an assessment is a requirement. Frequently, in the past, teachers decided what they were going to teach and then tried to design a test that would measure the success of that instruction. Teachers should instead design the assessment procedures informed by and reflecting criterion standards before instruction occurs. As Stiggins (2004) advocates, the teacher should continually assess the target, because the target *is* the criterion standard.

By giving students criterion-referenced assessments based on criterion standards, the teacher tests material taught in the curriculum on a regular and sustained basis. In addition, the teacher tests without paper and pencil. The regular activities of the class are used as a means of determining if a student is or is not reaching a criterion standard or target.

The results of criterion-referenced assessments must include more narrative than traditional letter grades. A simple A or B, P or F, or 75 or 90 percent cannot truly communicate what a student knows or can do. Chances are that criterion standards will be scored on a daily basis by handheld computers or card readers as technology increasingly finds its level in the classroom. Students cannot meet a standard half or three-quarters of the way. However, they may be half or three-quarters of the way toward meeting a standard. Rubrics using criterion standards can be designed for grading purposes that give criteria in the categories of "does not meet the standards," "meets the standards," or "exceeds the standards."

Assessment results should be utilized to (1) report progress to students and parents, (2) communicate a student's abilities to subsequent teachers, (3) inform businesses and postsecondary institutions of a given student's abilities, and (4) guide further instruction. Reporting progress to students and parents serves to keep them apprised with respect to where the student stands in the instructional process. Students, teachers, and parents all should have a basic understanding of where the student is at the beginning of the process and where he or she should be at the conclusion of instruction. Given these two landmarks, progress reporting becomes an analysis of the progress the student has made from point A toward point B.

In most cases, students move on to subsequent teachers or instructional processes, thus the postassessment from one level becomes the preassessment for the next. This allows the teacher of the next phase to get a clear picture of the student's strengths, weaknesses, and interests, enabling that teacher to plan appropriately. Since the criterion standards are written on a continuum basis from grade to grade and course to course, the teacher knows exactly how to appraise students at the beginning of a particular grade or course. The teacher can then refer to the criterion standards that should have been achieved to determine if the student is ready for the next level or phase of instruction.

Record Keeping on Handheld Computers

With the advent of handheld computers, teachers will be able to keep records of incidental student activities. In this way, assessment will not intrude upon learning. As a student demonstrates performance of one of the criterion standards, the teacher can note and file this information electronically. At the end of a grading period, the teacher can then call up the data and note, for example, that a student effectively achieved a criterion standard on five separate occasions.

Enhancing Teacher Performance

Several states, including Tennessee, Pennsylvania, Ohio, and others, have or are developing programs in *value-added assessment* (Hershberg, 2005). With this procedure, student improvement becomes the focus of teacher performance. The criterion standards can be used as the criteria to determine if students are improving. Each time a student achieves a criterion standard, that student is demonstrating improvement on a continuum of established, defined criteria.

Since this value-added system is being employed to measure teacher success, teacher supervision can be a much more meaningful process when standards are used to guide the supervisory process. Assuming the real intent of supervision is the improvement of the instructional process and the professional growth of teachers, supervisors can utilize standards to establish a common ground between teacher and supervisor. The role of supervision then becomes one of assisting the teacher to become adept at enabling students to achieve the criterion standards assigned to the teacher's course, unit, or lesson. This, of course, requires the supervisor to be thoroughly versed in standards, as well as ways and means of assessing these standards within the instructional process. To impose the old-fashioned supervisory model (designed to weed out teachers) is counterproductive and a waste of time and resources. Time and attention need to be on the end results: Can students demonstrate their achievement of criterion standards?

With criterion standards in place, teacher evaluation can become a matter of determining the teacher's proficiency in getting students to the accepted levels of success. How teachers do their jobs becomes less important than whether they are assisting students to achieve the standards. Consequently, forms used for observation and evaluation can be designed in a manner that reflects standards-based education.

A standards-based curriculum constructed using criterion standards makes teacher supervision more specific and practical. When an administrator observes a teacher using a standards-based curriculum, the administrator can observe from the perspective of the standards. The observer can determine very early in the lesson if the teacher is teaching to the curriculum, because the lesson plan and the early part of the lesson should cite the criterion standards that are the focus of the lesson.

A well-recognized and effective way of evaluating teacher performance is through an observation process that includes a preconference, an observation, and a postconference.

In the preconference, the teacher should do the following:

1. Articulate the standard and criterion standards that are addressed in the lesson.

2. Articulate assessment opportunities in which students can demonstrate progress toward achievement of criterion standards.

During the lesson, certain elements should be evident:

1. Does the teacher articulate the standards and criterion standards to be addressed in the lesson?

2. Is it evident that the lesson is related to the standards and criterion standards?

3. Does the teacher offer students opportunities to demonstrate progress toward achievement of the standard or criterion standards through active learning?

4. Does the teacher define the standards typically found in other academic disciplines that are also addressed in this lesson? For example, in a math class, does the teacher define the need to follow the "listen to others" standard? Or does the teacher tell students that they must "use complete sentences" on a science lab report?

5. Does the teacher establish assessment opportunities for students to demonstrate accomplishment of criterion standards?

6. Are criterion standards for the course visually evident? For example, are they listed on a poster on the classroom wall?

The postconference should focus on all aspects of the standards-based curriculum and instruction:

1. The observer should focus on each of the questions above and tell the teacher if she or he has offered a complete standards-based approach.

2. The observer should ask the teacher to explain his or her ideas for a summative assessment that will be given at some point concerning the standards.

Each school district usually has its own observation tool. If the questions listed above are made part of the tool, the teacher and observer have a view of what is happening in relation to standards. Also, teachers can self-evaluate with these questions. By reviewing the questions before and after teaching a lesson, teachers can gauge their own approaches to teaching in the standards-based mode.

Academic Freedom

Frequently, academic freedom becomes a topic of discussion when curriculum is written, because, in a sense, when curriculum is written, teachers are being told what they are expected to teach. By using criterion standards, teachers have the ultimate of academic freedom. First, criterion standards are written in a democratic manner, and all who wish are allowed to provide input into the process. Second, the process simply lays out realistic goals for students. As long as the teacher stays within the boundaries of good pedagogical practices and within the policies of the local school district, the teacher can use any means necessary to facilitate the achievement of the standards.

In a standards-based educational process, academic freedom is actually enhanced. Covering the text or material is no longer the measurement of teacher accomplishment. Rather, the goal is to have students demonstrate that they have acquired the desired knowledge and skills. How teachers get students to this point is, within reason, a matter of professional choice and judgment.

STANDARDS-BASED INSTRUCTIONAL PLAN: ENGLISH ■

Criterion standards should establish a pattern of learning that leads a student from basic knowledge to a use of that knowledge in practical situations. The plan may include criteria that, when standing alone, define a rubric for the lesson. Teachers who use daily assessment will be able to determine if students meet each component of the rubric by offering them opportunities to demonstrate achievement of these criteria. When a student can do this, all can be assured that the student has achieved the intent of the standards.

Note, in the following lesson plan, that the teacher defines criterion standards, so the student is expected to show practical use of knowledge, not simply take a test on knowledge. If a school or district has not defined criterion standards to accompany each of the state standards, teachers may create their own criterion standards to serve this purpose.

ENGLISH INSTRUCTIONAL PLAN

SOURCE: Bernadette Boerckel, Warrior Run School District

Unit: **Introduction to Mythology**

Grade: **9**

Course: **English**

Overview of the Unit

This grade nine English plan lays out the way that a school envisions the achievement of three standards. The expectations of how a student demonstrates achievement of the standards are stated as criterion standards. The reader knows exactly what this student is supposed to do in order to show that the standard is being achieved.

Standards Assessed in This Unit

- **1.2.8.** Read and understand essential content of informational texts and documents in all academic areas.
  - ☐ Identify essential information from several different electronic text sources about a mythological figure.
  - ☐ Reword appropriate information to concisely answer questions provided.
  - ☐ Combine reworded information into a unified presentation about a mythological figure with a beginning, a middle, and an end.

- **1.8.8.** Organize, summarize, and present the main ideas from research.
  - ☐ Demonstrate an understanding of information through appropriate visual representation.
  - ☐ Determine a logical order in which to present information.
  - ☐ Assess what information is most interesting and relevant to present.

- **3.7.10.** Apply basic computer operations and concepts.
  - ☐ Use a PowerPoint slide show to communicate research findings.
  - ☐ Create a presentation that utilizes space, color, animation, composition, and text appropriately.
  - ☐ Offer the slide show to class members in an oral presentation; observe the rules of public speaking previously addressed in class.

SOURCE for standards: Pennsylvania Department of Education, 2001

Teacher Activities and Instructional Techniques

1. The teacher provides models and direct instruction through the use of a PowerPoint illustration about one aspect of mythology.

2. The teacher uses strong questioning techniques that lead to student discussion.

3. The teacher demonstrates to students how she is going to grade student PowerPoint presentations.

Student Learning Activities

Introductory Activities

1. Students write down three things they think they know about mythology and three things that they would like to know. Discussion follows.

2. Students view a list of popular products and brand names that come from mythology.

3. Students generate a list of modern movies that are based on themes from ancient mythology (themes provided by teacher).

Class Work and Homework

1. Students discuss lists of products, name brands, themes, and characters whose origins are from mythology in order to understand mythology's relevance in life today.

2. Students define a list of vocabulary words from *Theseus and the Minotaur.*

3. Students read *Theseus and the Minotaur* aloud as a class as an example of a story in mythology and answer questions upon completion.

4. Students choose a mythological figure to research using the Internet.

5. Students create a PowerPoint presentation of at least six slides addressing the following prompts:
   a. Who is your mythological figure?
   b. What is he/she/it known for in mythology?
   c. Provide a detailed physical description.
   d. Tell a story involving him/her/it.
   e. Describe any powers connected to him/her/it.
   f. Does your figure have any relevance in today's society?

   The slide show should include at least one picture per slide and involve animation and sound.

6. Students will present their slide shows to the class orally, keeping in mind important elements of public speaking (volume, pace, posture, eye contact).

Measuring Achievement of Standards

Formative Assessment

1. Students receive credit for participating in initial group discussions.

2. Students write answers to comprehension questions from *Theseus and the Minotaur;* answers will be graded.

3. Students take a test on vocabulary definitions and spelling.

Summative Assessment

Each student presents a PowerPoint slide show with a minimum of six slides on a mythological figure. The presentation should

1. answer the six prompts provided above,

2. contain at least one picture per slide,

3. be aesthetically appropriate, and

4. use sound animation.

Public speaking skills will also be taken into consideration during the presentation.

Criterion Standards Rubric

1. The student *identified* essential information from several different electronic text sources. YES or NO

2. The student *reworded* appropriate information to concisely answer questions. YES or NO

3. The student *combined* reworded information into a unified presentation about a mythological figure with a beginning, a middle, and an end. YES or NO

4. The student *demonstrated* an understanding of information through appropriate visual representation. YES or NO

5. The student *determined* a logical order in which to present information. YES or NO

6. The student *assessed* what information was most interesting and relevant to present. YES or NO

7. The student *used* a PowerPoint slide show to communicate research findings. YES or NO

8. The student *created* a presentation that utilized space, color, animation, composition, and text appropriately. (See the additional presentation rubric under Summative *Assessment* above.) YES or NO

9. The student *shared* the slide show with class members in an oral presentation. The student observed the rules of public speaking previously addressed in class. YES or NO

5

Instructional Plans Based on Criterion Standards

Every classroom teacher can and should use standards as the basis for his or her instructional plans; criterion standards are the means by which this can be accomplished. Each component of the instructional plan relates directly to state standards as they have been articulated through criterion standards. The student learning activities, assessments, and criterion standard rubrics work together to help define an instructional strategy that is designed with a specific set of guidelines and expected criteria for success. It is up to the classroom teacher to determine through what means instruction will be provided and how knowledge will be demonstrated. The instructional plans found here, and at the ends of the other chapters, exemplify an easy-to-use format for developing instructional plans.

COMPONENTS OF THE INSTRUCTIONAL PLANS ■

Each instructional plan has a standard set of components. The principal components used in this method are discussed in the following paragraphs. A school could devise its own format for instructional planning, but this book makes very clear that standards and criterion standards must be the focus of the plan. Because of this, it is highly recommended that the standards are placed in a prominent position in the plan and that they stand out for the reader. Standards should never be placed on the second page of an instructional plan or positioned in any way that makes them appear to be an afterthought.

Overview of the Course or Unit

After the grade level, course, and unit have been identified, the overview provides a brief summary of why this material is being taught. The overview should employ an economical number of words. The purpose of the overview is to provide real-world statements as to why the instructional plan is being used. The overview should be composed so that a noneducator may read and understand the information.

Standards Assessed in This Course or Unit

These lessons present representative state standards to give the reader an idea of the material from which criterion standards and the lesson plans themselves can be derived. The reader will recognize the state standard because it is preceded by its number in bold print.

Each state has its own way of publishing standards and coding them. If the instructional planning format in this book is chosen for use by a local school, the school will need to determine how it chooses to make state standards recognizable. The purpose of the bold print and the coding in this method is to make sure that people not only mentally consider the importance of standards, but that they also see visual expression of the importance of the standards.

With one exception, all the state standards used as examples in the plans in this chapter are taken from the state of Pennsylvania's *Academic Standards* (Pennsylvania Department of Education, 2001). Some plans use an individual school's standards as well; the school's numbers for these standards are shown, but that they are not in bold face.

Criterion Standards to Be Assessed

These are derived from the state standards by constructing a verb matrix (see Chapter 3), or state standards may themselves serve as criterion standards, as shown in the first example. It is important to be sure that higher-level thinking skills are exercised and measured. The criterion standards should be designated in direct relationship to standards. The method employed here indents the criterion standard inside the margin of the standards and has a box-like bullet beside it. The bullets are box-shaped so that teachers can check off criterion standards as students demonstrate achievement of the standards defined by each statement.

Teacher Activities and Instructional Techniques

These are statements articulating what the teacher will do to deliver instruction and to evaluate student understanding in the midst of student discovery; it is hoped that evaluation can occur without interrupting learning. The statements found here should be limited to what the teacher *does as a teacher* and should never describe what is to be learned or what the student is supposed to do.

Student Learning Activities

These tasks are designed as a means for the students to gather information or work in a new way with information that they have previously gathered. It is through working in this way that students can make personal meaning from the material and transfer that knowledge to real-world situations. The student learning activities should be directly connected to the performances defined in the criterion standards. Some plans provide details of activities; others only brief summaries that teachers can use as an outline to define their own activities.

Measuring Achievement of Standards

During any instructional activity, the teacher must offer students an opportunity to demonstrate what they know and can do. This part of the plan should state the actual activities and experiences that students will have so that the teacher can determine if they are learning.

Criterion Standards Rubric

Not all lessons shown here include a rubric, because the criterion standards themselves can be used as the rubric, but some lessons offer a rubric set apart from the criterion standards. Here the teacher can indicate whether the student has evidenced mastery of the criterion standard through assessment, student learning activities, and summative assessment. Some of the rubrics use an evaluation system that requires simply circling *YES* or *NO* to indicate either that yes, the student has achieved this criterion standard, or no, the student has not yet achieved the criterion standard. Others include a point scale where the student can receive more points for demonstrating higher-order thinking skills than he or she does for displaying lower-order skills.

STANDARDS-BASED INSTRUCTIONAL PLANS ■

Each instructional plan shown in this book is but one opportunity for students to demonstrate their movement toward achieving a state or criterion standard. Students must be provided with multiple chances to meet standards throughout the course of their K–12 school careers. Therefore, there may be several instructional plans that include the same standards and criterion standards. Because of this, the reader will note that the teacher may have edited the literal criterion standard so that it reflects the particular lesson being shown.

The first plan is a yearlong plan devised for high school students who hope to meet the mathematics requirements for entry to a community college. This plan, developed by Bryan James—a mathematics instructor at the Pennsylvania College of Technology, and James Davis—an author of this book, shows how criterion standards aligned to state standards can define a full integrated mathematics course. The teacher's activities and instructional techniques have yet to be added to this plan.

MATHEMATICS INSTRUCTIONAL PLAN

Unit: **All Units**

Grade: **High School**

Course: **Topics in Mathematics MATH 153**

Overview of the Course

This course is intended as a general education course for students who will not major in mathematics or science in college. Topics will include geometry (points, lines, polygons, area, volume, and surface area), matrices, probability (sample spaces, counting techniques, conditional probability, odds), and statistics (measures of central tendency and dispersion, normal distribution, scatter plots). The emphasis is on the interconnection of mathematical concepts.

Standards Assessed in This Course

Geometry

- **2.9.8.B.** Illustrate, label, measure, and list properties of complementary, supplementary, and vertical angles.
  - ☐ **2.3.8.C.** Calculate angles in degrees and determine relations of angles.

- **2.9.8.C.** Identify familiar polygons as regular or irregular up to a decagon.
  - ☐ **2.9.8.D.** Identify, name, draw, and list all properties of squares, cubes, pyramids, parallelograms, quadrilaterals, trapezoids, polygons, rectangles, rhombi, circles, spheres, triangles, prisms, and cylinders.
  - ☐ **2.9.8.F.** Compare and contrast similar and congruent polygons.
  - ☐ **2.9.11.D.** Identify corresponding parts in congruent triangles to solve problems.
  - ☐ **2.9.11.J.** Analyze figures in terms of the kinds of symmetries they have.

- **2.9.11.I.** Illustrate situations geometrically to formulate and solve problems.
  - ☐ **2.3.8.A.** Develop formulas and procedures for determining measurements (e.g., area, volume, distance).
  - ☐ **2.3.8.D.** Estimate, use, and describe measures of distance, rate, perimeter, area, volume, weight, mass, and angles.
  - ☐ **2.3.8.B.** Develop solutions to rate problems (e.g., rate x time = distance, principal x interest rate = interest).

- **2.10.8.A.** Calculate measures of sides and angles using properties, the Pythagorean Theorem, and right triangle relationship.
  - ☐ **2.10.8.B.** Solve problems requiring indirect measurement for lengths of sides of triangles.
  - ☐ **2.10.11.B.** Identify, create, and solve practical problems involving right triangles using the trigonometric functions and Pythagorean Theorem.

- **2.10.11.A.** Use graphing calculators to display periodic and circular functions; describe properties of the graphs.

Matrices

- **2.8.11.D.** Develop expressions, equations, inequalities, systems of equations, systems of inequalities, and matrices to model routine and non-routine problem situations.
- **2.8.11.G.** Analyze and explain systems of equations, systems of inequalities, and matrices.
- **2.8.11.I.** Use matrices to organize and manipulate data, including matrix addition, subtraction, multiplication, and scalar multiplication.

Probability

- **2.7.11.B.** Apply probability and statistics to perform an experiment involving a sample and generalize the results to the entire population.
  - ☐ **2.7.08.B.** Illustrate the results of an experiment using visual representations (e.g., tables, charts, graphs).
  - ☐ **2.7.08.C.** Analyze predictions.
  - ☐ **2.7.08.E.** Determine valid inferences, predictions, and arguments based on probability.

- **2.7.11.A.** Compare and contrast odds and probability.
- **2.7.11.C.** Assess and justify a conclusion regarding the validity of a probability or statistical argument.
- **2.7.11.E.** Determine solutions to problems involving independent simple and compound events.

Statistics

- **2.6.8.A.** Compare and contrast different plots of data using values of mean, median, mode, quartiles, and range.
  - ☐ **2.6.8.C.** Fit a line to the scatter plot of two quantities and describe any correlation of the variables.
  - ☐ **2.6.8.E.** Analyze and display data in stem-and-leaf and box-and-whisker plots.

- **2.6.8.D.** Design and carry out a random sampling procedure.
  - ☐ **2.6.8.B.** Explain effects of sampling procedures and missing or incorrect information on reliability.
  - ☐ **2.6.11.H.** Use sampling techniques to draw inferences about large populations.

☐ **2.6.11.E.** Determine the validity of the sampling method described in a given study.

☐ **2.6.8.G.** Determine the validity of the sampling method described in studies published in local or national newspapers.

- **2.6.11.B.** Use appropriate technology to organize and analyze data taken from the local community.

  ☐ **2.6.8.F.** Use scientific and graphing calculators and computer spreadsheets to organize and analyze data.

- **2.6.11.D.** Explain predictions using interpolation, extrapolation, regression, and estimation using technology to verify them.

- **2.6.11.I.** Illustrate the normal curve and use its properties to answer questions about sets of data that are assumed to be normally distributed.

Student Learning Activities

The student should have the opportunity to complete the following:

1. Use geometry concepts in a variety of situations. Students should focus on angles, the measurement of angles, shapes, and volume of shapes in numerous situations. Students should demonstrate a comprehension of how angles relate to polygons and how various shaped objects are constructed and/or measured through geometric concepts.

2. Develop an understanding of the use and function of matrices. Students should be given the opportunity to interpret and construct matrices in the process of using numerical data.

3. Comprehend numerical probability and its importance to knowledge and problem solving. Students should learn to use probability data as a part of drawing conclusions from experiments done in classroom situations.

4. Examine the use of statistics in information systems. Students should develop a full comprehension of central tendency.

Measuring Achievement of Standards

The teacher will have numerous opportunities to observe the behaviors described in the state standards.

SCIENCE INSTRUCTIONAL PLAN

SOURCE: Amy Rosenbaum, Muncy School District

Unit: **Life Cycles Unit**

Grade: 3

Course: **Science**

Overview of the Unit

Students focus on the concept of the different life cycles of animals and plants.

Standards Assessed in This Unit

- **3.3.3.A.** Identify the similarities and differences of living things.
  - ☐ Compare and contrast complete and incomplete metamorphosis.
  - ☐ Explain the stages in the life cycle of a specific animal.
  - ☐ Classify the characteristics seeds must have in order to travel in different ways.

- **3.2.3.B.** Describe objects through scientific observations.
  - ☐ Assess the changes in the stages of the life cycle of the monarch butterfly from egg to adult.
  - ☐ Assess the changes in the stages of the life cycle of the cricket from egg to adult.
  - ☐ Through scientific observation, determine the similarities and differences between the life cycles of the monarch butterfly and the cricket.

- **1.8.3.C.** Organize and present the main ideas from the research.
  - ☐ Research and classify information regarding the stages of the life cycle of an animal.
  - ☐ Create a poster presenting information on the stages of the life cycle of an animal.
  - ☐ Present life cycle poster to the class.

Teacher Activities and Instructional Techniques

1. Read and discuss "Chapter 1: Life Cycle of Animals," *Discovery Works Life Cycles* (Ginn Science, 1999).

2. Read and discuss "Chapter 2: Life Cycle of Plants," *Discovery Works Life Cycles* (Ginn Science, 1999).

3. Discuss the differences between complete and incomplete metamorphosis.

Student Learning Activities

1. *Transformation Activity:* Students act out stages of metamorphosis for the following insects:
   - ☐ Honeybee
   - ☐ Yellow Jacket
   - ☐ June Beetle
   - ☐ Lady Bug
   - ☐ Japanese Beetle
   - ☐ Butterfly
   - ☐ Mosquito
   - ☐ Lacewing
   - ☐ Luna Moth
   - ☐ Fly
   - ☐ Ant

2. *Seed Traveling Activity:* Groups of students read about seeds traveling on water or wind, by using animals, or by hitchhiking. They then write, and share with the class, the characteristics seeds need in order to travel using a particular method.

3. *Growth Observation:* Students raise monarch butterflies and crickets as a class and observe the stages of growth in their life cycles by taking measurements and recording observations.

4. *Life Cycle Research:* Using classroom materials, library materials, or the Internet, students research the life cycle stages of a ladybug, hummingbird, green snake, fighting fish, chicken, wood frog, jumping spider, or horse.

5. *Posters:* Students create posters presenting the following information about the animal they researched:
   a. Life cycle stages
   b. Characteristics at each stage
   c. Habitat of the animal
   d. What the animal eats and drinks
   e. A surprise fact about the animal

The checklist below will help students keep track of their findings.

Life Cycles Checklist

Research: You will need to answer these questions through your research.

_____ 1. What are the stages of growth that your animal goes through? (What are its life cycle stages?)

_____ 2. What are the characteristics of each stage of the life cycle? For example,
   - ☐ What does the animal look like at each stage?
   - ☐ What does the animal act like at each stage?

_____ 3. What is the habitat of the animal? (Where does it live? In a forest? Underground? Somewhere else?)

_____ 4. What does your animal eat and drink?

_____ 5. Find a surprise fact about your animal that you don't think anyone will know.

Measuring Achievement of Standards

Preassessment

What do students know about the life cycles of animals? What do students know about the life cycles of plants?

Formative Assessment

1. Observe active participation in discussions.

2. Observe correct actions in transformation activity.

3. Assess seed traveling activity using a rubric.

4. Assess student records of observations of monarch butterflies and crickets using a checklist.

5. Assess life cycle posters and presentations using checklists and rubrics.

6. Assess by giving an animal life cycle test.

7. Assess by giving a plant life cycle test.

Criterion Standards Rubric

1. The student correctly compared and contrasted complete and incomplete metamorphosis. YES or NO

2. The student correctly explained the stages in the life cycle of a specific animal. YES or NO

3. The student correctly classified the characteristics seeds must have in order to travel in different ways. YES or NO

4. The student correctly assessed the changes in the stages of the life cycle for the monarch butterfly from egg to adult. YES or NO

5. The student correctly determined the similarities and differences between the life cycles of the monarch butterfly and the cricket. YES or NO

6. The student researched and correctly classified information regarding the stages of the life cycle of an animal. YES or NO

7. The student created a poster presenting information on the stages of the life cycle of an animal. YES or NO

8. The student gave an oral presentation describing his or her life cycle poster project. YES or NO

MATHEMATICS INSTRUCTIONAL PLAN

SOURCE: Rob Wallis, Muncy School District

Unit: Perimeter, Circumference, Area

Grade: 6

Course: **Mathematics**

Overview of the Unit

This unit allows students to discover the meaning and application of perimeter, circumference, and area. Students use computers to construct polygons that are used to represent a miniature golf course.

Standards Assessed in This Unit

This school has defined its own set of standards in relation to state standards. For each state standard, the school's standards are listed, as well as the school's criterion standards.

- **2.3.8.A.** (1) Model and explain using manipulatives (e.g., string, square, and cubes), linear measure, area, and volume. (2) Measure and apply formulas for perimeter and area for these polygons: rectangle, triangle, parallelogram, and circle. (3) Apply formulas for volume for rectangular prisms and cylinders.
  - ☐ Identify the perimeter/circumference and area of a given polygon.
  - ☐ Utilize formulas to find the area of rectangles, triangles, parallelograms, and circles.
  - ☐ Compose an essay explaining the solution to a real-world predictable problem involving perimeter and area.

- **2.9.6.C.** (1) Identify, draw, label, and classify regular polygons up to decagon. (2) Identify, draw, and label circles, chords, and arcs.
  - ☐ Use a protractor, compass, and straightedge efficiently and effectively.
  - ☐ Explain the differences between radii, diameters, and chords.
  - ☐ Construct various polygons when given the perimeter/circumference and area.

- **3.6.7.B.** Identify and use information technologies used for encoding, transmitting, receiving, storing, and decoding information.
  - ☐ Identify technologies that could be used to construct polygons.
  - ☐ Utilize illustration technology to effectively and efficiently draw polygons.
  - ☐ Compose a three-paragraph essay explaining the obstacles encountered while using technology to construct polygons and the strategies used to overcome those obstacles.

Teacher Activities and Instructional Techniques

1. Preassessment on polygons up to a decagon, triangles, circle components, perimeter, area, and circumference formulas.

2. Lecture on perimeter, area, and circumference.

3. Lecture on radii, diameters, and chords.

4. Lecture on use of a straightedge, compass, and protractor and on construction of angles.

5. Lecture on circular compass (360°) and construction of angles and polygons.

Student Learning Activities

1. Groups solve perimeter, area, and circumference problems.

2. Groups solve problems involving radii, diameter, and chords.

3. Individual students construct congruent angles and polygons by employing straightedges, compasses, and protractors efficiently and effectively.

4. Using a straightedge, compass, and protractor, students design a miniature golf hole that will be added to a new course in their area.

5. Students work in groups, pairs, and alone to utilize computer programs that can draw polygons of differing shapes and sizes.

6. Students individually select a computer program and then construct several different polygons (both those assigned by the teacher and personal choices).

7. Students write a three-paragraph essay about the difficulty or ease of the program used.

8. Students get back into groups and swap essays with partners. Students teach their partners how to use their preferred programs, sharing difficulties of the programs and strategies used to solve them.

Measuring Achievement of Standards

Criterion Standards Rubric

Use the following checklist to identify student success:

1. ____The student can identify the perimeter/circumference and area of a given polygon.

2. ____The student can utilize formulas to find the area of rectangles, triangles, parallelograms, and circles.

3. ____The student can use a protractor, compass, and straightedge efficiently and effectively.

4. ____The student can explain the differences between radii, diameter, and chords.

5. ____The student can construct various polygons when given the perimeter/circumference and area.

6. ____The student can identify technologies that could be used to construct polygons.

7. ____The student can utilize illustration technology to effectively and efficiently draw polygons.

8. ____The student can compose an essay explaining the solution to a real-world predictable problem involving perimeter and area.

9. ____The student can compose a three-paragraph essay explaining the obstacles encountered while using technology to construct polygons and strategies used to overcome those obstacles.

10. ____The student uses correct punctuation and grammar in all writing.

Scoring Guide:

10 checks	=	100%
9 checks	=	94%
7–8 checks	=	88%
5–6 checks	=	76%
4 or fewer checks	=	Reteach and Reassess

ENGLISH INSTRUCTIONAL PLAN

SOURCE: Angela Dupes, Midd-West School District

Unit: **Exploring Career Choices**

Grade: **9**

Course: **English**

Overview of the Unit

At four separate times throughout the year, students research and write about possible career choices.

Standards Assessed in This Unit

- **1.8.11.B.** Locate information using appropriate sources and strategies.
  - ☐ Identify five important keywords that can be used in conjunction with electronic search tools, such as electronic card catalogs and Internet search engines.
  - ☐ Name one book source and one Internet source that might be used to collect information about a chosen career.
  - ☐ Employ at least two sources to gather information about a selected career, such as duties, required education, skills, and abilities.

- **1.5.11.B.** Write using well-developed content appropriate for the topic.
  - ☐ Identify both who the audience is and whether informal or formal language should be used for a paragraph about a chosen career.
  - ☐ Compose a paragraph that both identifies and explains four skills that are required for a chosen career.
  - ☐ Compose a paragraph that assesses whether the student's current abilities, interests, accomplishments, and aptitudes are conducive to the career choice.

- **13.1.11.B.** Analyze career options based on personal interests, abilities, aptitudes, achievements, and goals.
  - ☐ State one possible career interest.
  - ☐ List four skills that are necessary in the chosen career.
  - ☐ Assess whether the career choice is a possibility based on current abilities, interests, accomplishments, and aptitudes.

Teacher Activities and Instructional Techniques

The teacher asks the following set of questions:

1. What four careers are you most interested in?

2. Why are you interested in each of these careers?

3. What skills do you think are required for these particular careers?

Students write responses to these questions in a journal.

Student Learning Activities

1. Students select one career that they are interested in researching.

2. Students brainstorm five keywords that are related to this career choice. They write the career choice and keywords on a piece of paper.

3. In the library, students use their five keywords in both a card catalog search and an Internet search using the search engine of their choice. (If students' keywords do not yield the information they are looking for, they refine their keywords until they receive favorable results.)

4. Students explore all sources that the keywords uncover and select at least one book source and one Internet source.

5. From the two discovered sources, students take notes on career information. The notes for the career must contain the following items: duties of individuals employed in the chosen career, required education, and at least four skills or abilities.

6. Students use their notes on their chosen careers to create a four-square. (This is a visual, prewriting activity.) In this four-square, students identify the proper audience and language required for their writing activity, write an introduction of their chosen career, expand on the four skills required for the career, and compare and contrast their skills and abilities to those of the chosen career.

7. Using the four-square, students compose three paragraphs about their career exploration. The first paragraph introduces the chosen career and explains why it was selected. The second paragraph identifies and explains four of the skills that are required for this career, and the third paragraph compares and contrasts the students' knowledge, skills, and abilities with those required by the career.

Measuring Achievement of Standards

During the unit, the teacher observes students and checks to see if each one is able to do the following:

1. Name four career choices.

2. Identify five appropriate keywords for research.

3. Utilize resources to gather required information about the career (duties, education, and skills and abilities needed).

4. Determine personal skills, abilities, accomplishments, and aptitudes.

5. Compose developed paragraphs that use appropriate language and detail and are specific to an intended audience.

Criterion Standards Rubric

1. The student named four possible career interests. YES or NO

2. The student identified five usable keywords to search for career information. YES or NO

3. The student utilized research resources to gather required information. YES or NO

4. The student determined which personal skills, abilities, accomplishments, and aptitudes coincided with his or her career choice. YES or NO

5. The student composed paragraphs that were audience- and detail-specific. YES or NO

EARTH SCIENCE INSTRUCTIONAL PLAN

SOURCE: Daniel S. Jury, Montoursville Area School District

Unit: **Water Cycle**

Grade: 7

Course: **Earth Science**

Overview of the Unit

"A Rain Drop Fairy Tale" is a writing assignment given to students in Earth Science to assess their understanding of the water cycle, as well as of recurring patterns and narrative writing.

Standards Assessed in This Unit

- **3.1.7.C.** Identify different patterns as repeated processes or recurring elements in science and technology.
  - ☐ Identify the parts of the water cycle.
  - ☐ Compare the parts of the water cycle to other processes studied, such as the rock cycle.
  - ☐ Infer the impact of the water cycle on the Earth's surface.

- **3.5.7.D.** Explain the behavior and impact of the Earth's water systems.
  - ☐ Deduce the reasons for evaporation, condensation, precipitation, and runoff.
  - ☐ Compare and contrast the processes of evaporation and condensation.
  - ☐ Develop a diagram of the water cycle.

- **1.4.8.A.** Write short stories, poems, and plays (cross-curricular standard).
  - ☐ Relate the action of the water cycle to common fairy tales.
  - ☐ Draw analogies between the water cycle and the characters of a fairy tale.
  - ☐ Utilize the good writing techniques of focus, content, organization, style, and conventions.

Teacher Activities and Instructional Techniques

1. Provide students with discovery activities to elucidate the processes involved in the water cycle, such as evaporation, condensation, precipitation, and runoff.

2. Direct students in the diagramming or modeling of the water cycle.

3. Make sufficient formative assessment through homework review exercises and in-class inquiry to determine student learning progress.

Measuring Achievement of Standards

A student's score is the sum of his or her points as determined by the table below.

Criterion Standards Rubric

Table 5.1

	Points Awarded				
Criterion	4	3	2	1	0
Proper Length	Story is at least one page handwritten on every line, or one page typed, double-spaced, in 12-point type.	Story is less than one page, but greater than three-quarters of a page in length.	Story is between three-quarters and one-half page in length.	Story is less than one-half page in length.	Student did not attempt to write story.
Score on Pennsylvania Writing Rubric	Story scores an average of between 3.6 and 4.0 on the rubric.	Story scores between 3.0 and 3.5 on the rubric.	Story scores between 2.5 and 2.9 on the rubric.	Story scores between 1.0 and 2.4 on the rubric.	Student did not attempt to write story.
Creativity	Student draws analogy between drops of water and the characters of a fairy tale; there is unique dialogue and action that parallels the processes of the water cycle.	Student draws analogy between drops of water and the characters of a fairy tale; there is some action that parallels the processes of the water cycle.	Student draws analogy between drops of water and the characters of a fairy tale; there is little to no action, yet more than just a summary of the water cycle.	Student draws no analogy between drops of water and the characters of a fairy tale; student provides no more than a summary of the water cycle.	Student did not attempt to write story.
Scientific Detail	Student includes the four main processes of the water cycle (evaporation, condensation precipitation, and runoff) with supporting details.	Student includes the four main processes of the water cycle but provides no supporting details.	Student includes two or three of the four main processes of the water cycle, with or without supporting details.	Student includes fewer than two of the four main processes of the water cycle, with no supporting details.	Student did not attempt to write story.

SOCIAL STUDIES INSTRUCTIONAL PLAN

SOURCE: Michael D. Sundberg, Mifflinburg Area School District

Unit: **Designing Your Dream House**

Grade: **11**

Course: **Consumer Economics**

Overview of the Unit

Students assess the factors involved in making consumer housing decisions. They demonstrate their knowledge by creating an analysis and written description of a dream house that meets their needs and utilizes the appropriate consumer information.

Standards Assessed in This Unit

- **11.1.12.C.** Analyze the relationship among factors affecting consumer housing decisions (e.g., human needs, financial resources, location, legal agreements, maintenance requirements).
  - ☐ List the individual needs for a place to live for yourself.
  - ☐ Gather information on three different sources of mortgages, and compare the interest rates and conditions of the loans.
  - ☐ Assess the pros and cons of three different locations for building a house.

- **11.1.12.F.** Compare and contrast the selection of goods and services by applying effective consumer strategies.
  - ☐ Develop a list of furniture to buy to furnish a house, and estimate the cost.
  - ☐ Determine which interest rate and loan would be best for your situation.
  - ☐ Construct and analyze a plan on how to reduce the overall costs of moving into a new home (secondhand furniture, moving costs, installation costs, etc.).

- **1.4.11.B.** Write complex informational pieces (e.g., research papers, analyses, evaluations, essays; cross-curricular standard).
  - ☐ Compose a written description of your dream house, identifying how the elements of the house (layout, furniture, design, etc.) meet your needs.
  - ☐ Describe in detail the location of your house, and cite three specific reasons as to why this location was chosen over the other two locations.
  - ☐ Create a chart or table comparing mortgage rate choices, and assess the best choice for your situation.

Teacher Activities and Instructional Techniques

The teacher techniques in this instructional unit involve all things articulated in the assessment portion of this plan. The teacher uses some direct instruction in the introduction.

Introduction: Discuss housing options with students. Discuss lenders and types of mortgages, such as fixed-rate, adjustable-rate, and balloon-rate mortgages. Discuss some possible ways of attaining home furnishings and services.

Student Learning Activities

Students participate in discussion, complete the research, and complete a project. Research directions include the following:

1. Compile a list of your own housing needs and wants.

2. Using the Internet, conventional paper sources, or personal interviews, gather mortgage rates and information from three different sources.

3. Using the Internet, conventional paper sources, and personal interviews, identify the cost of furniture, moving, and living on your own.

4. Investigate options for locations of homes using varied sources.

Measuring Achievement of Standards

Preassessment

What are the costs involved in buying a house? Where would you go to get a mortgage for a house?

Criterion Standards Rubric

1. The student determined and identified his or her individual needs in regard to choosing a place to live. YES or NO

2. The student compiled data on interest rates and terms of loans from three different sources. YES or NO

3. The student identified three different locations for building the house and the pros and cons of each. YES or NO

4. The student constructed a list of articles to furnish a house and correctly estimated the cost of the items. YES or NO

5. The student compared data collected on mortgages and assessed the most appropriate choice for the situation. YES or NO

6. The student developed a plan to minimize the costs of moving. YES or NO

7. The student composed a written description of the dream house that met the expected criteria. YES or NO

8. The student effectively explained the choice of location and the rationale for the choice. YES or NO

9. The student correctly used relevant graphics to show mortgage-rate options and final choice. YES or NO

INDUSTRIAL TECHNOLOGY INSTRUCTIONAL PLAN

SOURCE: Jeff Lorson, Jersey Shore Area Middle School

Unit: **Recycling**

Grades: **6–8**

Course: **Technology Education**

Overview of the Unit

This unit allows students to use the Seven-Step Design Process to design and build an automated can crusher according to certain design constraints. The challenge is to build a working prototype of an automatically feeding aluminum can crusher that reduces the volume of the can by a minimum of 70 percent. The problem is researched, and then several possible solutions are brainstormed. From those, the most feasible solution is built using the tools and materials called out by the bill of materials. The solution is then evaluated to determine its efficiency, speed, and feasibility in the commercial world.

Standards Assessed in This Unit

- **3.2.12.D.** Analyze and use the technological design process to solve problems.
  - ☐ Assess all aspects of the problem, prioritize the collected information, and formulate five potential problems that must be answered before the solution can be implemented.
  - ☐ Propose, develop, and appraise the best solution, and determine the two best alternative solutions.
  - ☐ Evaluate and assess the design solution, and make a minimum of two improvements to the original solution.
  - ☐ Identify a minimum of three positive and three negative effects of the design solution on society.

- **3.7.12.A.** Apply advanced tools, materials, and techniques to answer complex questions.
  - ☐ Demonstrate safe use of a minimum of five complex tools and machines within their specifications.
  - ☐ Apply both linear and circular interpolation to a Computer Numeric Control milling machine program that will fit into the design solution.

- **2.3.11.C.** Demonstrate the ability to produce measures with specified levels of precision.
  - ☐ Determine appropriate levels of tolerances according to the parts designed for the solution.
  - ☐ Demonstrate proper use of four different measurement instruments.
  - ☐ Produce a part from an engineering drawing that is within specified tolerances.

Teacher Activities and Instructional Techniques

Preassessment: Identify the level of competency that each student has in the design process, in the use of tools and materials, and in measurement.

Provide a Design Brief: "You are part of a group of engineers working for the Jersey Shore Aluminum Works. Your company just received a letter from the ALCOA, who buys your recycled aluminum cans, stating that your company must reduce the volume of its scrap aluminum cans by 70 percent or they will receive 30 percent less per pound to recycle them. Due to this potential decrease in profit, the CEO of your company has given your group this challenge: Using the Seven-Step Design Process, design and build an automated can crushing machine that has the capability to reduce the volume of your cans by 70 percent and also to crush 60 cans per minute."

Facilitation of Learning: Focus on students who are struggling with a concept in a certain area on an as-needed basis. Learning is student-directed, unless deadlines are not being met.

Student Learning Activities

Research: Students conduct research using the Internet as well as the school library and the Pennsylvania Power Library, all of which can be accessed through any computer in the school lab.

Schedule of Events: Students develop a schedule of key events that identifies when each part of the project will need to be completed in order to have a desirable solution by the scheduled due date.

Measuring Achievement of Standards

Each student keeps a portfolio in which check marks and teacher initials are written as the student shows competency in each standard. All criterion standards are reviewed with each student at the end of the unit to ensure that she or he has retained mastery of the skills learned during the unit.

COMPUTER TECHNOLOGY INSTRUCTIONAL PLAN

SOURCE: Charles Greco, Columbia-Montour Area Vocational-Technical School

Unit: **PC Maintenance and Repair—The Motherboard**

Grade: **High School**

Course: **PC Maintenance and Repair**

Overview of the Unit

In this unit, students learn about

- different types of motherboards.
- the various components on motherboards.
- how to install a motherboard.
- how to troubleshoot motherboard problems.
- how to research specifications for a motherboard online.

In addition to Pennsylvania state standards, this plan uses task standards as defined for the PC maintenance and repair program in this school.

Standards Assessed in this Unit

- **Task F005.** After reading section from the text, identify the four popular types of motherboards used in today's personal computers.
  - ☐ Describe major differences between the types of motherboards.
  - ☐ Explain when one type of motherboard would be used in place of another.

- **Task F006.** List the main components found on a typical motherboard.
  - ☐ Identify processor, socket, expansion slots, chip set, BIOS chip, and other specified components.
  - ☐ Explain the differences in these components using two different lab motherboards.

- **Task F007.** Demonstrate proper motherboard installation technique utilizing the lab exercise found in the student lab manual.
  - ☐ Given an empty computer case, properly mount and secure a motherboard.

- **Task F008.** Troubleshoot common motherboard problems.
  - ☐ Troubleshoot errors intentionally created on the motherboard by the instructor.

- **1.8.11.B.** Locate information using appropriate sources and strategies.
  - ☐ Determine valid resources for researching the topic, including primary and secondary resources.
  - ☐ Evaluate the importance and quality of the sources.

Teacher Activities and Instructional Techniques

1. Class lecture with corresponding PowerPoint presentation

2. Instructor-led lab exercises

Student Learning Activities

1. Reading

2. Completion of textbook questions

3. Note taking

4. Hands-on lab exercises

5. Internet research

6. Writing assignment

Measuring Achievement of Standards

1. Evaluation of written responses to questions

2. Examination of students hands-on labs

3. Evaluation of written research assignment

BIOLOGY/CHEMISTRY/HEALTH INSTRUCTIONAL PLAN

SOURCES: James Ulrich and Debra Fern, Warrior Run High School; Linda Hoover, Susquehanna Community Career and Technical Center

Unit: **Cells and Tissues With Related Membranes**

Grade: **High School**

Course: **Anatomy and Physiology (Biology)**

Overview of the Unit

Students gain an understanding that molecules make up the fabric of living cells, which, in turn, make up tissues. Students learn the role of adhesion molecules, the classification of tissues, and the various cell types found in tissues.

Standards Assessed in This Unit

- **3.2.12.C.** Compare and contrast the structure and function of the four major tissue types.
  - ☐ Identify all likenesses and all differences among the four tissue types.
  - ☐ Break down the structure of the tissue types by relating the function to the structure.
  - ☐ Appraise how one malfunctioning tissue type will affect the other three tissue types.

- **3.3.12.A. (AP 1.5).** Identify locations of various accessory organs and layers of skin.
  - ☐ Name the locations and layers when asked to do so.
  - ☐ Use an illustration to identify the locations of varied organs.
  - ☐ Demonstrate this knowledge when using computer dissection.

- **3.3.12.A. (AP 1.4).** Determine the difference between fiber types and the matrix of tissues where they are found.
  - ☐ In a computer lab, define the fiber types and identify where they are found.
  - ☐ Explain the matrix of tissues while examining a graphic sample on the computer.
  - ☐ Identify the differences between the fiber types while completing the computer lab.

- **3.3.12.B.** Identify the components of a cell and determine their function within the cell.
  - ☐ Illustrate a cell on a paper drawing.
  - ☐ Explain the function of each cell component when presenting to the class.

☐ Demonstrate knowledge of cell components, and analyze each component's function in answers given in class discussion.

- **R11.A.2.** Understand nonfiction text appropriate to grade level.
  ☐ Identify core facts and knowledge of reading assignments.
  ☐ Retell information read in the text and other resources.
  ☐ Develop summary statements concerning all reading assignments.

SOURCE for standards: Indiana Department of Education, 2006

Teacher Activities and Instructional Techniques

The teacher reads, lectures, questions, and facilitates labs and discussions.

Student Learning Activities

Students read for information, define new terms, use microscopes, participate in discussions, create concept maps, complete study guides, and complete appropriate labs.

Measuring Achievement of Standards

Achievement is measured through tests, quizzes, lab activities, worksheets, homework, and classroom participation.

TELECOMMUNICATIONS INSTRUCTIONAL PLAN

SOURCE: Donna Harris, Columbia-Montour Area Vocational-Technical School

Unit: **Telephone Communication Skills**

Grade: **High School**

Course: **Hotel and Tourism**

Overview of the Unit

Students achieve a basic understanding of different telephone services. Students learn how to take and receive messages with little error. In addition to Pennsylvania state standards, this plan uses task standards as defined for the hotel and tourism program in this school. In this plan, the teacher has created an outline of her overall standards; a state standard and the school's task standards are used as criterion standards within her outline.

Standards Assessed in This Unit

- Read and comprehend "Telephone Services" in the textbook.
  - ☐ Identify three of the five different types of telephone service.
  - ☐ Describe the differences among types of services.
  - ☐ Fill out the assigned workbook pages to demonstrate knowledge.

- Demonstrate sending and receiving messages using telephones.
  - ☐ E.3.01. Answer the phone with a smile on your face.
  - ☐ E.3.02. Use a low-pitch voice.
  - ☐ E.3.03. Speak clearly and slowly.
  - ☐ Avoid expressions such as "uh-huh" and "yeah."

- Demonstrate written messages with full understanding.
  - ☐ E.3.04. Write the caller's full name.
  - ☐ E.3.05. Identify the date and time of the call.
  - ☐ E.3.06. Restate the caller's phone number.
  - ☐ Compose a message for the person who missed the call.
  - ☐ E.3.07. Do not abbreviate; provide a full message.

- **1.6.11.C.** Speak using skills appropriate to formal speech situations.
  - ☐ Use a variety of sentence structures to add interest to a presentation.
  - ☐ Pace the presentation appropriately for the audience and purpose.
  - ☐ Demonstrate an awareness of the audience.

Teacher Activities and Instructional Techniques

The teacher role-plays a situation that includes giving and receiving important information. The teacher conducts class discussions about receiving correct information.

Student Learning Activities

These include writing, listening, proper responses, and manners.

Measuring Achievement of Standards

The teacher evaluates students in a real-life situation when students are answering the classroom phone.

6

Lesson Planning
Takes Root

Teachers use what is expected of students (defined as criterion standards) as the root of the lesson plan. Once all state standards have been reduced to grade-level criterion standards in all subject areas, the result is a comprehensive district curriculum of expectations, not courses. This type of curriculum is significantly different from a course map. This type of curriculum literally lets teachers, students, parents, and community members know what is expected of students as opposed to what courses students must "pass." With a listing of criterion standards for each course in the secondary level and each grade and subject in the elementary level, there is a descriptive tool to define what a student must actually know and be able to do at the end of the course or the year.

The Brockway Area School District in Pennsylvania has defined these criterion standards for all K–12 programs. To show parents and teachers what is expected of first graders, they used the criterion standards as part of a planned course document. Figure 6.1 on the next page shows the planned course document for first grade mathematics. Note that state standards are preceded by their numbers in bold type.

Figure 6.1 Planned Course Document

BROCKWAY AREA SCHOOL DISTRICT

Date of Adoption:	**[to be written in by teacher]**
Course:	**Mathematics**
Grade:	**1**
Length of Time to Complete Course:	**one school year**

Objective

Students develop an understanding of numerical concepts and relationships.

Overview of Course

During this course, students focus on counting to 100, addition and subtraction, geometry and fractions, graphing, place value, money, telling time, and measurement. Students count by ones, twos, fives, and tens to 100. They identify place value up to 100. Students will also learn to graph using varied forms of graphing.

Students demonstrate addition and subtraction facts to 18. They add and subtract one- and two-digit numbers with no renaming. They read word problems, write equations, and solve problems from the word problems. Students solve addition facts using strategies such as doubles and doubles plus one. They solve subtraction facts using the guess and check strategy, addition, and related addition double facts.

Students identify and draw plane shapes and three-dimensional shapes. They identify parts of shapes in relation to fractions. Students use the metric and English systems of measurement to estimate and measure. Students count change to a quarter. They tell time to the hour and half hour, recognizing five-minute increments.

Resources

- Scott Foresman-Addison Wesley Grade 1 workbooks
- Assorted teacher-enrichment kits as supplied by Scott Foresman-Addison Wesley
- Concrete manipulative objects
- Trade books
- Overhead transparencies

Measuring Achievement of Objectives

The basis of assessment is the framework established by the Pennsylvania Academic Standards as adopted from January of 2000 through August of 2003 and the Pennsylvania Anchor Standards as issued in May of 2004. Teachers focus on the various standards within the academic area and the anchor standards across the curriculum.

In this course, the following Pennsylvania academic standards and assessment anchors are the focus of assessment:

2.1. Numbers, Number Systems, and Numbering Relationships

2.2. Computation and Estimation

2.3. Measurement and Estimation

2.5. Mathematical Problem Solving and Communication

2.9. Geometry

R.3.A.2. Reading Assessment Anchor

(Continued)

Figure 6.1 (Continued)

These types of assessments will be used:

The teacher's individual assessment by observation

The teacher's oral questioning and responses

Students' responses to questions on basic worksheets as supplied by the Scott Foresman–Addison Wesley books

Students' responses to fill-in-the-blank tests supplied by Scott Foresman–Addison Wesley

Standards Assessed in This Course

By the end of this course, a student should be able to achieve the following standards:

- **2.1.A.03.01.b.** Demonstrate counting by ones, twos, fives, and tens to 100 orally.
- **2.1.3.B.** Identify parts of shapes and groups as fractions.
- **2.1.C.03.01.a.** Demonstrate numbers from 1–100 using tens and ones place value blocks.
- **2.1.C.03.01.b.** Demonstrate whole numbers in various ways (1, one, 2–1, 0+1, etc.) through the use of concrete objects, drawings, word names, and symbols.
- **2.1.D.03.01.a.** Identify equal parts using drawings, diagrams, or models to show the concept of fraction or part of a whole.
- **2.1.E.03.01.c.** Calculate change from a quarter.
- **2.1.L.03.01.a.** Demonstrate knowledge of basic facts in addition to 18.
- **2.1.L.03.01.b.** Demonstrate knowledge of basic facts in subtraction from 18.
- **2.2.A.03.01.d.** Identify the correct operation (+,-) to solve a word problem using concrete objects or by drawing a picture to demonstrate understanding.
- **2.2.3.B** Solve single- and double-digit addition and subtraction problems with regrouping in vertical form.
- **2.3.B.03.01.c.-d.** Use a ruler to measure the length of an object in inches and centimeters.
- **2.3.B.03.01.f.** Utilize cups, pints, quarts, and liters to determine the capacity of a container.
- **2.3.D.03.01.c.** Use a manipulative clock to show a given time to the hour and half hour.
- **2.5.A.03.01.a.** Demonstrate the ability to solve word problems using one of a variety of problem-solving strategies (e.g., draw a picture, use a problem-solving guide, use manipulative objects).
- **2.9.A.03.01.a.** Identify plane and solid shapes.
- **2.9.C.03.01.a.** Demonstrate the ability to identify a triangle, square, or rectangle with manipulatives or pictures.
- **R3.A.2.** Demonstrate the ability to understand and interpret mathematics problems appropriate to grade level.
- **R3.A.2.1.** Identify the meaning of vocabulary from mathematics.
- **R3.A.2.3.** Make inferences and draw conclusions based on the numbers found in mathematics situations.
- **S4.A.1.3.1.** Observe and record change by using time and measurement.
- **S4.A.1.3.2.** Describe relative size, distance, or motion using numbers and number operations when working with these kinds of problems.
- **S4.A.2.1.4.** State a conclusion that is consistent with the information/data found in one of the mathematics problems.

SOURCES for standards: Pennsylvania Department of Education, 2001, 2005

Several points are worth considering about the potential of the planned course document shown in Figure 6.1. First, the reader will see that the language of each statement is designed in the context of what happens in the Brockway district in first grade. Each of these statements is contextual and clear to teachers. Second, the academic boundaries are not confined to mathematics. Instead, criterion standards from reading and science are used in this document. The belief is that students will not succeed in mathematics unless they can reason with language and use mathematics in science contexts.

If a school uses the criterion standards in a map form, teachers can see the vertical and horizontal relationships of learning expectations. In Figures 6.2, 6.3, and 6.4, the reader can see illustrations of how a curriculum map of criterion standards could be designed. These types of maps would provide educators with a tool that would require them to view learning expectations from the perspectives of various subject areas and of more than one grade. The vertical and horizontal learning expectations would be evident to all.

Figure 6.2   Criterion Standards for One State Standard at Two Grade Levels

State Standard: 2.6.A. Gather, organize, and display data using pictures, tallies, charts, bar graphs, and pictographs.	
Grade Level	Criterion Standard
1	**2.6.A.03.01a.** Identify the number of days of sunshine, clouds, or rain on a class-constructed pictograph showing the weather for one month.
2	**2.6.A.03.02a.** With a partner, create a bar graph showing days of sunshine, clouds, or rain for one month.

Figure 6.3   How One Criterion Standard Addresses Standards in Language Arts, Math, and Science

School Subject	State Standard	Criterion Standard
Language Arts	**1.6.E.03.01.** Participate in small and large group discussions and presentations.	**1.6.E.03.01.a.** Identify and discuss weather each day and participate in creating a classroom graph showing the local weather for a month to determine patterns.
Mathematics	**2.6.A.** Gather, organize, and display data using pictures, tallies, charts, bar graphs, and pictographs.	**2.6.A.03.01.a.** Identify and discuss weather each day and participate in creating a classroom graph showing the local weather for a month to determine patterns.
Science	**3.1.C.03.01.** Illustrate patterns that regularly occur and reoccur in nature.	**3.1.C.03.01.a.** Identify and discuss weather each day and participate in creating a classroom graph showing the local weather for a month to determine patterns.

Figure 6.4   Criterion Standards for One State Standard in Five Different Subjects

State Standard: 1.4.B.03. Write informational pieces (e.g., descriptions, letters, reports, instructions) using illustrations when relevant.	
Subject	*Criterion Standard*
Language Arts	**1.4.B.03. a.** Write a friendly letter to a classmate; then identify the parts of a letter.
Mathematics	**1.4.B.03. b.** Explain the way to find the perimeter of a rectangle.
Science	**1.4.B.03. c.** Write a report about a planet to present to the class.
Social Studies	**1.4.B.03. d.** Create a report about a favorite president.
Geography	**1.4.B.03. e.** Write instructions on how to identify common rocks.

INTEGRATING THE CURRICULUM ■

Implications for Supervision

As discussed in Chapter 4, subject area supervisors or department chairpersons find it especially helpful to print out and examine the vertical perspective (between grade levels) of the curricular map that relates to their subject areas. Doing so makes it possible to supervise from the standpoint of subject area standards. Thus, supervisors and their teachers can continually fine-tune their curriculum by filling in gaps, culling irrelevant material, and adding emergent concepts to their subject areas.

The horizontal perspective (across curriculum) from two or more subject areas can be compared by supervisors and teachers. They can identify areas of common concern. They can also discuss strengthening the application and reinforcement of their respective subjects through work in other disciplines. For instance, tenth grade teachers could sit down with their horizontal slice of this map and determine interdisciplinary units that most efficiently help students achieve the standards. This can save precious instructional time by reducing duplication of efforts.

Just as awareness of the responsibility at each grade level for preparation for the next level promotes learning and optimizes instructional time, so does the interdisciplinary integration of traditional subject areas. The criterion standards make it much easier to identify skills and knowledge that cut across subject areas. For example, the Civil War as a theme for instruction can carry through to a number of subject areas beyond its usual place in the social science curriculum. For example, students may study literature produced during or about the Civil War, statistics and demographics from the 1860s, or the art and music of that historical period. Each subject has criterion standards that can be processed through a Civil War theme. The horizontal communication process during the writing of criterion standards brings to light possible interdisciplinary relationships. In addition, the performance aspect of the criterion standards (signaled by a performance verb) encourages different subject-area teachers to collaborate on their instructional activities. Assessment tasks are excellent opportunities to integrate subjects when projects are used that require students to demonstrate communication skills while using knowledge of other subject areas to complete the task. (Such assessment tasks can also be instructional tasks, of course.)

Criterion standards require teachers to view curriculum from the perspective of what students know and can do, and dialogue among colleagues is required to accomplish this. Dialogue will enable teachers to see how they can integrate concepts, teach to standards, and prepare students for state tests. Discussion greatly increases the efficiency of instruction, as teachers learn to eliminate duplication of efforts and actually begin to build on each other's accomplishments. Teachers see that students not only need to write across the curriculum; students must also learn across the curriculum by meeting all standards in all subject areas.

■ THE PLANNED COURSE DOCUMENT

The primary reason for rendering curriculum into manageable pieces (criterion standards) is to guide daily instruction in the classroom. To spend numerous hours and dollars to produce a curriculum document that simply gathers dust on a shelf or satisfies state mandates is an extreme waste of resources. One method for making curriculum accessible and highly usable is the *planned course document,* such as the one shown in Figure 6.1. The planned course document is a condensed version of a yearlong lesson plan. It comprises information about every aspect of the course, including resources used, a course description, instructional activities, state standards and the corresponding criterion standards, as well as an assessment plan.

Planned course documents produced using criterion standards should be used on a daily basis. Since the criterion statements are descriptions of what students must know and be able to do, the planned course document gives the teacher an activity and assessment plan for the year. Teachers should keep their criterion standards on their desks and refer to them frequently as they prepare their daily lessons.

Further, teachers can use planned course documents to communicate to students and parents about the content and objectives of their courses. The documents also make excellent handouts to all students at beginning of each course. Planned course documents using criterion standards serve to keep teachers and students focused on the tasks at hand. They also guide assessment by communicating to students what they should be able to do as a result of a particular segment of instruction.

The map model shown in Figure 6.5 shows how individual grade levels and subject content areas can be integrated within a planned course document. There are many aspects to the map model. There is a total curriculum map that represents a profile of the graduating student or the districtwide curriculum. There is the vertical slice that depicts the subject area responsibilities, and the horizontal slice that delineates grade-level responsibilities.

What Is in a Name?

Throughout the course of writing curriculum with standards and criterion standards, teachers and administrators will no doubt be struck by the fact that this approach requires people to look at strands or concepts that run from kindergarten level to graduation. The reality is that much of what educators are asked to address does not fit into neat little subject packages

Figure 6.5   Curricular Mapping With Criterion Standards

Curricular Mapping With Criterion Standards

Grade level	Language Arts	Mathematics	Science	Social Studies	
Kindergarten					
lst Grade		Horizontal Slice			
2nd Grade					
3rd Grade					
4th Grade					
5th Grade					
6th Grade					
7th Grade					
8th Grade					
9th Grade					
10th Grade					
11th Grade					
12th Grade					

Planned Course Document

Course Title:

Resources Used:	Course Description:	Instructional Activities:

Standard	Standard	Standard	Standard	Standard	Standard
Criterion Standards	Criterion Standards	Criterion Standards	Criterion Standards	Criterion Standards	Criterion Standards

Assessment:

BETWEEN GRADE LEVELS

Vertical Slice

ACROSS CONTENT AREAS

(contrary to how courses and curriculum have been designed in the past). The disjointed nature of curriculum is due to the packaging of courses along traditional lines. For example, when we package algebra as a course, the implication is that algebra has nothing to do with geometry. Nothing could be farther from reality. Much of what is required in achieving the standards for geometry is dependent on algebraic concepts. Therefore, it may make sense to call courses "math K" to "math 12" instead of calling them by more compartmentalized terms like algebra or geometry. If the standards and the criterion standards were used to define what students are supposed to know and be able to do, a school could develop a series of units of instruction that might lead to more in-depth understanding of material.

■ DEVELOPING THE STANDARDS-BASED INSTRUCTIONAL PLAN

The purpose of using a standards-based instructional plan is twofold. It gives the teacher a way of focusing on what students are supposed to know and be able to do, and it gives the teacher a way of documenting that standards are being utilized in the classroom. Instructional plans can be designed so that teachers are focused on what students are supposed to know and do, not on what the teacher is supposed to cover. If a planned course is based on criterion standards, there can be numerous ways that the teacher can plan for the student to demonstrate ability to achieve a standard.

Instructional plans based on criterion standards include some very basic information concepts found in traditional planning. The plan must show the teaching techniques, the assessment techniques, the resources used to support the instruction, and the student learning activities. The focus of the plan, however, must be on the standards and criterion standards.

In order to concentrate on standards in instructional planning, the learning expectations must be the primary focus of the plan. The teacher can start the plan by naming the lesson or unit, composing a very brief overview, and determining the resources to be used. At this point, the teacher must determine the standards and criterion standards that will be the heart of learning in this plan. Once the standards are determined, the teacher can devise the remaining part of the plan.

If teachers are given an opportunity to develop teaching techniques and student learning activities first, there is a strong possibility that coverage of information and completion of student activity, as opposed to achievement of standards, will be the focus of the lesson By contrast, when teachers are required to consider the standards and what is expected of students to achieve the standards, all teaching techniques and learning activities can be deliberate functions of the steps necessary for achievement. It is imperative that the plan be designed around standards and criterion standards.

It is clear that state education agencies are holding school districts accountable for student achievement of standards. Too often the results of state tests are the only evidence used to determine if a student has achieved the standards and by extension if the teachers have successfully taught them. The strategy of formulating criterion standards and then creating daily lesson plans, planned courses, and districtwide curriculum around the criterion standards enables teachers to prove that they teach to the standards. Through the use of criterion standards, a student's class work is predictive of his or her performance on the state test. Each lesson provides an opportunity for students to show what they know or do not know, which in turn gives the teacher a chance to fill in gaps in student understanding. Criterion standards tie state standards to classroom practice, creating a means for students to get on and stay on the right educational track.

STANDARDS-BASED INSTRUCTIONAL PLAN: ■
LEARNING SUPPORT–LANGUAGE ARTS

The following lesson is designed for special needs students. The reader will note that a cross-curricular approach is used throughout the plan. This could not be accomplished easily or efficiently if the teacher were not able to find the standards and related criterion standards on some form of criterion standard map.

LANGUAGE ARTS INSTRUCTIONAL PLAN FOR SPECIAL NEEDS STUDENTS

SOURCE: Crissy M. Walker, Williamsport Area School District

Unit: **Detour Through the Digestive System**

Grade: **6**

Course: **Learning Support—Language Arts**

Overview of the Unit

Students research the path food takes through the digestive system. They demonstrate their knowledge by writing a story about their trip through the digestive process.

Standards Assessed in This Unit

- **E.2.a.** The student will produce a report that includes appropriate facts and details.
  - ☐ Compose a written report describing the path food takes through the digestive system.
  - ☐ Proofread your own writing or the writing of others, using dictionaries and other resources, including the teacher or peers as appropriate.
  - ☐ Use proper grammar, spelling, and punctuation.

- **S.2.a.** The student will understand structure and function in living systems, such as the complementary nature of structure and function in cells, organs, tissues, organ systems, whole organisms, and ecosystems.
  - ☐ List steps in the digestive process in the written report.
  - ☐ Describe the function of specific digestive organs as part of the written report.
  - ☐ Use a drawing within the written report to demonstrate the path food takes from when it enters the body until it exits.

- **A.3.b.** The student will use information technology to assist in gathering, analyzing, organizing, and presenting information.
  - ☐ Use the Internet to research the digestive system.
  - ☐ Use graphic organizers found online to organize information before writing.
  - ☐ Conduct an independent study using human anatomy software.

SOURCES for standards: Pennsylvania Department of Education, 2001; Williamsport Area School District, personal communication, April 15, 2004

Teacher Activities and Instructional Techniques

Preassessment: KWL chart—What the students *know,* what they *want* to learn, and what they have *learned* (with *learned* column filled out after completion of unit).

Discussion: What are the steps in the writing process? How many sentences are in a good paragraph? What goes in a good introduction and conclusion? Discuss Pennsylvania System of School Assessment (PSSA) writing rubric.

Technology: Check out Web sites prior to student search. Install human anatomy software on appropriate number of computers. Review and discuss proper use of computers. Show students how to search on Internet. Discuss how to tell if a site is reliable.

Writing: Explain that students will be expected to compose an essay with a minimum length of five paragraphs using information found in their research.

Student Learning Activities

All student activities are articulated in the criterion standards.

Measuring Achievement of Standards

The students' final writing assignment will be graded using the PSSA writing rubric:

1. Focus—The single controlling point made with an awareness of task about a specific point.

   4   3   2   1

2. Content—The presence of ideas developed through facts, examples, details, opinions, reasons, and/or explanations.

   4   3   2   1

3. Organization—The order developed and sustained within and across paragraphs using transitional devices and including introduction and conclusion.

   4   3   2   1

4. Style—The choice, use, and arrangement of words and sentence structure that create tone and voice.

   4   3   2   1

5. Conventions—Grammar, mechanics, spelling, usage, and sentence formation.

   4   3   2   1

SOURCE for rubric: Pennsylvania Department of Education, 2002

Resources

- Internet sites designated by the teacher
- Human anatomy software
- Illustrations of the digestive system
- Graphic organizers

Resource A

Relevant Web Sites

Developing Educational Standards (http://edstandards.org/Standards .html), posted by the Wappingers Central School District of New York, offers an up-to-date view of each state's concern with standards. This site provides information from every state education agency in relation to the standards issue. By searching the links on the page, the searcher will see that many states have actually posted or made it possible to download the standards that they have constructed. All 50 states are represented, and there are links to many other sites related to the standards issue.

Other valuable sites that provide information on standards and curriculum include the following:

- American Federation of Teachers:
  http://www.aft.org/edissues/ standards

- Center for Educational Reform:
  http://edreform.com/standard.htm

- The Center for Performance Assessment:
  http://www.makingstan dardswork.com

- *Education Week* online journal:
  http://www.edweek.org

- Explore a Source:
  http://www.explorasource.com

- James Daniel Associates:
  http://www.jamesdanielassociates.com

- Assessment Training Institute:
  http://www.assessmentinst.com

- Understanding by Design:
  http://www.ascd.org/portal/site/ascd/menuitem.b66696ac45f924addeb3ffdb 62108a0c

Resource B

Verb Matrix Survey Material

Verb matrix survey materials are presented here so that readers may use them to develop their own verb matrices at the local level.

■ SURVEY QUESTION USED TO DETERMINE THE VERB MATRIX: *KNOW*

Below is the definition of *know* as stated in *Webster's New Collegiate Dictionary*. Please read the definition carefully.

Know: To have direct cognition of information.

Please place a check beside the one word illustration that you think best fits what a student can do when the student *knows* something.

A student has direct cognition when the student

_____ 1. Can communicate information or complete a learning activity without reference to external sources.

_____ 2. Can use memory as the only source to answer a question or complete the steps of a task.

_____ 3. Can repeat information or complete steps of a process without the use of any resource other than his or her mind and body.

_____ 4. None of the above statements is an acceptable illustration of the meaning of *know*.

If a student is expected to *know* something, which of the verbs below would best be used when asking the student to demonstrate that he or she knows the information or task process? Please circle the five verbs that you believe best illustrate the expectation.

arrange	show	choose	pick
omit	hold	select	find
cite	offer	group	recite
quote	tally	spell	label
underline	point to	list	say
identify	transfer	touch	match
reset	write	name	sort
locate	repeat	check	tell

SURVEY QUESTION USED TO DETERMINE ■
THE VERB MATRIX: *COMPREHEND*

Below is the definition of *comprehend* as stated in *Webster's New Collegiate Dictionary*. Please read the definition carefully.

Comprehend: To grasp the nature, significance, or meaning of information.

Please place a check beside the one word illustration that you think best fits what a student can do when the student *comprehends* something.

A student grasps the nature, significance, or meaning of information when the student

_____ 1. Can present information in his or her own words or illustrations.

_____ 2. Can inform others of the information without repeating the information verbatim.

_____ 3. Can re-create the information with a different set of words or another form of illustration.

_____ 4. None of the above statements is an acceptable illustration of the meaning of *comprehend*.

If a student is expected to *comprehend* something, which of the verbs below would best be used when asking the student to demonstrate that he or she comprehends the information or task process? Please circle the five verbs that you believe best illustrate the expectation.

alter	explain	retell	change
render	outline	construct	restate
construe	qualify	spell out	define
expound	vary	translate	expand
convert	infer	moderate	transform
reword	account for	annotate	

■ SURVEY QUESTION USED TO DETERMINE THE VERB MATRIX: *APPLY*

Below is the definition of *apply* as stated in *Webster's New Collegiate Dictionary*. Please read the definition carefully.

> **Apply:** To put information to use, especially for practical purposes.

Please place a check beside the one word illustration that you think best fits what a student can do when the student *applies* something.

A student uses information when the student

_____ 1. Can utilize external information in the process of solving a problem or creating a concept.

_____ 2. Can relate external information to a process from start to finish.

_____ 3. Can rely on the external information to find answers to problems or create new ideas or products.

_____ 4. None of the above statements is an acceptable illustration of the meaning of *apply*.

If a student is expected to *apply* something, which of the verbs below would best be used when asking the student to demonstrate that he or she applies the information or task process? Please circle the five verbs that you believe best illustrate the expectation.

adopt	use	utilize	exploit
exert	exercise	manipulate	relate
put to use	wield	mobilize	devote
take up	try	make use of	ply
consume	capitalize on	put in action	
operate	handle	solve	
profit by	employ	avail	

SURVEY QUESTION USED TO DETERMINE ■ THE VERB MATRIX: *ANALYZE*

Below is the definition of *analyze* as stated in *Webster's New Collegiate Dictionary*. Please read the definition carefully.

> **Analyze:** To study or determine the nature and relationship of the parts by separating the whole into its component parts.

Please place a check beside the one word illustration that you think best fits what a student can do when the student *analyzes* something.

A student studies or determines the nature and relationship of the parts of a piece of information when the student

_____ 1. Can separate the various details within a piece of information and can communicate how each detail relates to other details in order to form the piece of information.

_____ 2. Can identify the respective parts and communicate how the parts relate to other parts in the context of the whole piece of information.

_____ 3. Can communicate what each part is and can communicate how each part facilitates the message delivered by the whole piece of information.

_____ 4. None of the above statements is an acceptable illustration of the meaning of *analyze*.

If a student is expected to *analyze* something, which of the verbs below would best be used when asking the student to demonstrate that he or she analyzes the information or task process? Please circle the five verbs that you believe best illustrate the expectation.

assay	scrutinize	screen	sift
look into	inspect	uncover	test for
take apart	syllogize	survey	dissect
include	examine	reason	check
deduce	study	simplify	
section	search	breakdown	
canvas	divide	audit	

■ SURVEY QUESTION USED TO DETERMINE THE VERB MATRIX: *SYNTHESIZE*

Below is the definition of *synthesize* as stated in *Webster's New Collegiate Dictionary*. Please read the definition carefully.

Synthesize: To combine or produce through composing parts or elements so as to form a whole.

Please place a check beside the one word illustration that you think best fits what a student can do when the student *synthesizes* something.

A student produces a piece of information by combining parts and elements when the student

_____ 1. Can develop a piece of information by composing respective details into an entity with self-identity.

_____ 2. Can create an idea by composing several parts and elements into one piece of information.

_____ 3. Can combine new pieces of information with old pieces of information to form an original idea.

_____ 4. None of the above statements is an acceptable illustration of the meaning of *synthesize.*

If a student is expected to *synthesize* something, which of the verbs below would best be used when asking the student to demonstrate that he or she synthesizes the information or task process? Please circle the five verbs that you believe best illustrate the expectation.

blend	make	formulate	mature
compose	combine	produce	breed
effect	reorganize	cause	conceive
make up	create	form	evolve
yield	generate	originate	structure
compile	reorder	build	
develop	construct	constitute	

SURVEY QUESTION USED TO DETERMINE THE VERB MATRIX: *EVALUATE*

Below is the definition of *evaluate* as stated in *Webster's New Collegiate Dictionary*. Please read the definition carefully.

Evaluate: To determine or fix the value of something.

Please place a check beside the one word illustration that you think best fits what a student can do when the student *evaluates* something.

A student determines or fixes the value of something when the student

_____ 1. Can support his or her opinion with relevant information.

_____ 2. Can communicate information that provides documentation for the value or significance of something.

_____ 3. Neither of the above statements is an acceptable illustration of the meaning of *evaluate*.

If a student is expected to *evaluate* something, which of the verbs below would best be used when asking the student to demonstrate that he or she evaluates the information or task process? Please circle the five verbs that you believe best illustrate the expectation.

adjudge	assay	arbitrate	grade
determine	rule on	judge	assess
weigh	decree	settle	censure
prioritize	umpire	classify	referee
award	criticize	reject	decide
rate	rank	appraise	

Bibliography

Alabama Department of Education. (n.d.). *Courses of study.* Retrieved January 12, 2005, from http://www.alsde.edu/html/CoursesOfStudy.asp

American Association of School Administrators. (1999). *Preparing school and school systems for the 21st century.* Arlington, VA: American Association of School Administrators.

American Federation of Teachers. (November, 1999). *Educational issues policy brief number 11: Making standards matter.* Washington, DC: Author.

American Federation of Teachers. (1999/2000). Here to stay: Standards-based reform is not just another fad—it's alive, well, and living in the classroom [Electronic version]. *American Teacher, December/January.* Retrieved March 7, 2006, from http://www.aft.org/pubs-reports/american_teacher/dec99jan00/heretostay.html

Ames, N., & West, T. (1999). *Practices and strategies: Schools in the middle.* Reston, VA: National Association of Secondary School Principals.

Association of School Administrators. (1999). *Preparing school and school systems for the 21st century.* Arlington, VA: American Association of School Administrators.

Barell, J. (1998). *PBL: An inquiry approach.* Thousand Oaks, CA: Corwin Press.

Bloom, B. S., Englehart, M. D., Furst, E. J., Hill, W. H., & Krathwohl, D. R. (Eds.). (1956). *Taxonomy of educational objectives: Handbook 1, cognitive domain.* New York: McKay.

Bracey, G. W. (1994). *Transforming America's schools: An Rx for getting past blame.* Alexandria, VA: American Association of School Administrators.

Bromley, A. (2004). Standardized testing here to stay. *Inside UVA* [Electronic version]. Retrieved December 1, 2005, from http://www.virginia.edu/insideuva/2004/20/index.html

Burke, K. (1994). *How to assess authentic learning.* Thousand Oaks, CA: Corwin Press.

Buttram, J. L., & Waters, T. (1997). Improving America's schools through standards-based education. *NASSP Bulletin, (81)*590: 1–6.

Carr, J., & Harris, D. (2001). *Succeeding with standards: Linking curriculum, assessment, and planning.* Alexandria,, VA: Association for Supervision and Curriculum Development.

Collins, J. (2001). *Good to great: Why some companies make the leap and others don't.* New York: HarperCollins.

Colorado Department of Education. (2005). *Colorado K-12 academic standards.* Retrieved December 15, 2005, from http://www.cde.state.co.us/index_stnd .htm

Costa, A. (1999). Mediative environments: Creating conditions for intellectual growth. In B. Z. Presseisen (Ed.), *Teaching for intelligence I: A collection of articles.* Arlington Heights, IL: SkyLight.

Daggett, W. R. (1994). *Defining excellence for American schools.* Rexford, NY: International Center for Leadership in Education.

Daggett, W. R. (1995). *Testing and assessment in American schools—committing to rigor and relevance.* Schenectady, NY: International Center for Leadership in Education.

Daggett, W. R. (2000). *The curriculum matrix.* Rexford, NY: International Center for Leadership in Education.

Daggett, W. R. (2003). School counselors and information literacy from the perspective of Willard Daggett. *Professional School Counseling, 6*(4), 238–242.

Daggett, W. R., & Kruse, B. (1997). *Education is not a spectator sport.* Schenectady, NY: International Center for Leadership in Education.

Developing Educational Standards. (2006). Retrieved March 21, 2006, at http://edstandards.org/Standards.html

English, F. (1999). *Deciding what to teach and test: Deciding, aligning, and auditing curriculum* (Millennium Ed.) Thousand Oaks, CA: Corwin Press.

Farkas, S., Johnson, J., & Duffett, A. (2003). *Rolling up their sleeves: Superintendents and principals talk about what's needed to fix public schools.* New York: Public Agenda.

Florida Department of Education. (2005). *Sunshine state standards.* Retrieved March 1, 2006, from http://www.firn.edu/doe/curric/prek12/frame2.htm

Fogarty, R. (1991). *The mindful school: How to integrate the curricula.* Palatine, IL: SkyLight.

Friedman, T. (2005). *The world is flat: A brief history of the twenty-first century.* New York: Farrar, Straus, and Giroux.

Fullan, M. (2000). The three stories of education reform. *Phi Delta Kappan, 81*(8), 581–584.

Gagne, R. M., Briggs, L. J., & Wagner, W. W. (1988). *Principles of instructional design* (3rd ed.). New York: Holt, Rinehart, and Winston.

Gandal, M. 1995. Not all standards are created equal. *Educational Leadership, 52*(6), 16–21.

Ginn Science. (1999). *Discovery works life cycles.* Morristown, NJ: Silver Burdett Ginn.

Guskey, T. (2005). Mapping the road to proficiency. *Educational Leadership, 63*(3), 32–38.

Harris, K. (2004, November). *Personalizing instruction.* Paper presented at the meeting of the National Career Academy Coalition Conference, Santa Fe, New Mexico.

Hershberg, T. (2005). Value-added assessment and systematic reform: A response to the challenge of Human Capital Development. *Phi Delta Kappan, 87*(4), 276–283.

Illinois State Board of Education. (2005). *Illinois learning standards.* Retrieved March 6, 2006, from http://www.isbe.state.il.us/ils

Indiana Department of Education. (2006). *Indiana's academic standards.* Retrieved March 6, 2006, from http://www.doe.state.in.us/standards/welcome.html

Jacobs, H. H. (1997). *Mapping the big picture.* Alexandria, VA: Association for Supervision and Curriculum Development.

Jacobs, H. H. (Ed.). (2004). *Getting results with curriculum mapping.* Alexandria, VA: Association for Supervision and Curriculum Development.

Kendall, J. S., & Marzano, R. J. (1995). The McREL Database: A tool for constructing local standards. *Educational Leadership, 52*(6), 42–47.

Kendall, J. S., & Marzano, R. J. (1996). *Content knowledge: A compendium of standards and benchmarks for K–12 education.* Aurora, CO: Mid-continent Regional Educational Laboratory.

Killion, J. (1999). *Standards provide opportunity for staff development.* Oxford, OH: National Staff Development Council.

Kovalik, S. (1997). *Integrated thematic instruction: The model* (3rd ed.). Kent, WA: Books for Educators.

Linder, D. (2002). *The Scopes trial: An introduction.* Retrieved December 1, 2005, from http://www.law.umkc.edu/faculty/projects/ftrials/scopes/scopes.htm

Marzano, R. J. (2003). *What works in schools: Translating research into action.* Alexandria, VA: Association for Supervision and Curriculum Development.

Marzano, R. J., & Kendall, J. S. (1995). *Content knowledge: A compendium of standards and benchmarks for K–12 education.* Aurora, CO: Mid-continent Regional Educational Laboratory.

Marzano, R. J., & Kendall, J. S. (1996). *A comprehensive guide to designing standards-based districts, schools, and classrooms.* Alexandria, VA: Association for Supervision and Curriculum Development.

Marzano, R. J., McTighe, J., & Pickering, D. (1993). *Assessing student outcomes: Performance assessment using the dimensions of learning model.* Alexandria, VA: Association for Supervision and Curriculum Development.

Massachusetts Department of Education. (2005). *Curriculum framework.* Malden, MA: Massachusetts Department of Education.

McNamee, G., & Chen, J. (2005). Dissolving the line between assessment and teaching. *Educational Leadership, 63*(3), 72–77.

McTighe, J. (1995). *Developing performance assessment tasks for the classroom: Templates for designers.* Frederick, MD: Maryland Assessment Consortium.

McTighe, J. & Thomas, R. (2003). Backward design for forward action. *Educational Leadership, 60*(5), 52–55.

National Council on Education Standards and Testing. (1992). *Raising standards for American education.* Washington, DC: U.S. Department of Education.

Nebraska Department of Education. (n.d.) *Academic standards.* Retrieved March 6, 2006, from http://www.nde.state.ne.us/ndestandards/AcadStand.html

O'Shea, M. (2005). *From standards to success: A guide for school leaders.* Alexandria, VA: Association for Supervision and Curriculum Development.

Peckham, M. (1979). *Explanation and power: The control of human behavior.* New York: Seabury Press.

Pennsylvania Department of Education. (2001). *Academic standards.* Retrieved March 6, 2006, from http://www.pde.state.pa.us/stateboard_ed/cwp/view.asp?A=3&Q=76716

Pennsylvania Department of Education. (2002). *Handbook for report interpretation: 2002 PSSA writing assessment for grade 11.* Harrisburg, PA: Author.

Pennsylvania Department of Education. (2005). *Assessment anchors.* Retrieved December 8, 2005, from http://www.pde.state.pa.us/a_and_t/site/default.asp

Perna, D. (1997). *Using trigger verbs to merge curriculum and assessment in a school district curriculum design.* Unpublished doctoral dissertation, NOVA Southeastern University, Fort Lauderdale, FL.

Perna, D., & Davis, J. (1999). Facilitating the design of a standards-based curriculum. *Learning & Media, 25*(5), 22–24.

Public Agenda. (2003). *America's principals and superintendents—railing against a torrent of local, state, and federal mandates.* Retrieved March 21, 2006, from http://interversity.org/lists/arn-l/archives/Nov2003/msg00263.html

Quellmalz, E. (1991). Developing criteria for performance assessments: The missing link. *Applied Measurement in Education, 4*(4), 319–332.

Reeves, D. B. (2000). *Accountability in action: A blueprint for learning organizations.* Denver, CO: Advanced Learning Press.

Reyna, V. F. (1987). Easy extension, hard comprehension. In A. Ellis (Ed.), *Progress in the psychology of language.* Hillsdale, NJ: Lawrence Erlbaum.

Rudalevige, A. (2003). *The politics of No Child Left Behind.* Stanford, CA: Hoover Institution.

Saint Edward's University Center for Teaching Excellence. (2001). *Task oriented question construction wheel based on Bloom's Taxonomy.* Retrieved January 15, 2006, from http://www.stedwards.edu/cte/resources/bwheel.htm

Schmoker, M. (2000). The results we want. *Educational Leadership, 57*(5), 62–65.

Schmoker, M. (2001, October 24). The Crayola curriculum. *Education Week.* Retrieved December 1, 2005, from http://mikeschmoker.com/articles.html

Schmoker, M. (2002). Up and away. *Journal of Staff Development, 23*(2), 10–13.

Schmoker, M. (2003). First things first: Demystifying data analysis. *Educational Leadership, 60*(5), 22–24.

Schmoker, M., & Marzano, R. J. (1999). Realizing the promise of standards-based education. *Educational Leadership, 56*(6), 17–21.

Shikellamy School District. (1995). *Communications curriculum draft.* Sunbury, PA: Author.

Shikellamy School District. (1995). *Science and technology curriculum draft.* Sunbury, PA: Author.

South Carolina Department of Education. (2005). *Content area web pages.* Retrieved November 1, 2005, from http://www.myscschools.com/offices/cso

Spring, J. (2006). *American education* (12th ed.). New York: McGraw-Hill.

Squires, D. (2005). *Aligning and balancing the standards-based curriculum.* Thousand Oaks, CA: Corwin Press.

Stiggins, R . (2004). *Student-involved assessment for learning* (4th ed.). Upper Saddle River, NJ: Prentice Hall.

Stiggins, R. (2005). From formative assessment to assessment FOR learning: A path to success in standards-based schools. *Phi Delta Kappan, 87*(4), 324–328.

Texas Education Agency. (2005). *Texas essential knowledge and skills.* Retrieved November 1, 2005, from http://www.tea.state.tx.us/teks

Third International Mathematics Society Study (TIMSS). (1996). *Mathematics achievement in the middle school years.* Chestnut Hill, MA: TIMSS International Study Center.

Udelhofen, S. (2005). *Keys to curriculum mapping: Strategies and tools to make it work.* Thousand Oaks, CA: Corwin Press.

University of Maryland University College. (2005). *Using Bloom's Taxonomy in assignment design.* Retrieved January 15, 2006, from http://www.umuc.edu/ugp/ewp/bloomtax.html

West Virginia Department of Education. (n.d.). *WV content standards and objectives.* Retrieved November 1, 2005, from http://wvde.state.wv.us/csos

Wiggins, G. (1993). *Assessing student performance: Exploring the purpose and limits of testing.* San Francisco: Jossey-Bass.

Wiggins, G., & McTighe, J. (2005). *Understanding by design* (expanded 2nd ed.). Alexandria, VA: Association for Supervision and Curriculum Development.

Wiles, J., & Bondi, J. (2002). *Curriculum development: A guide to practice* (6th ed.). Upper Saddle River, NJ: Merrill Prentice Hall.

Williams, R. B., & Dunn, S. E. (2000). *Brain-compatible learning for the block.* Arlington Heights, IL: Corwin Press.

Williamsport Area School District. (2004, April 15). Personal communication.

Index